90 DAY
Journey
WITH THE
DEVIL

GOD STILL PERFORMS MIRACLES

WELDON BARNES

ISBN 978-1-63630-304-8 (Paperback)
ISBN 978-1-63630-305-5 (Digital)

All scriptures were quoted from the New King James Version Bible and the New International Version Bible.

Covenant Books, Inc.
11661 Hwy 707
Murrells Inlet, SC 29576
www.covenantbooks.com

I would like to dedicate this book to my beautiful wife Deborah Lee (Leavelle) Barnes. She has been my helper, my supporter, my rock, for over forty-seven years. I haven't made it easy for her at times, and I want her to know that if it had not been for her dedication to our marriage vows, and her Christian faith, we wouldn't have ever made it this far. We've had many good times, along with many trying times along the way.

I think the episode that I went through, not only strained our marriage, but strained her sanity. For that, I am truly sorry, but for all of her good qualities, and sticking with me for forty-seven years, I want to say thank you to my lovely wife.

I know God pairs people up for his purpose, and both of us will tell you that our marriage has not been all roses, but I'm thankful that God allowed me to have a partner and helpmate, as special as my wife.

A lot of women, not knowing how to handle a situation like I went through, wouldn't have stuck it out, nor had a clue how to seek help for me. Through her faith, and God's guidance, she amazed me how well she handled the crisis.

That is only a small part of my appreciation for my wife. She's been through the thick and thin, the good times and the sorrows over these forty-seven years. It takes a lot of giving and taking to make a marriage work that long, and I'll admit she's done a lot more giving than I have.

I dedicate this book to her and want to express my gratitude and tell her that I love her very much.

A very special thanks to Sandra Colbert, Martha Larson, Rylee Barnes and Deborah Barnes for helping me with punctuations and proofing. After reading this book you'll find out how much of an English scholar that I am not.

CONTENTS

INTRODUCTION

This book is about my life's journey, and the many different adversities that God has brought me through. How he has been working behind the scenes throughout my life, even though I wasn't even aware of it until later in life. As I've gotten older things are much clearer to me, of what all God has done for me and my family. When you're young, as life is happening, at the time things just seemed to work out at times. Those "seeming to work out periods of my life" was God working things out for me.

The reason this book is being written is because of a particular experience that I had in the spring of 1992. I was thirty nine years old and it was so bizarre that I still cannot explain, or understand exactly what happened to me.

What I will tell you, as you read this book, there will be some things that are very strange and probably unbelievable to some. Until this experience happened I didn't believe in some of these things myself, but with God's help I am going to explain it as honestly, and as truthfully as I can. Some of it will sound unbelievable and I don't blame you for feeling that way. Some people will think that I still need to be on medication or in a mental institution for some of my thoughts.

As you read through this book you will soon determine by my awkward way of phrasing things and my country slang, that I am not a professional writer. As a matter of fact other than a few newspaper articles, this is the only thing I've written at all. I am a farmer-rancher and if it weren't for my girlfriend's help I would not have passed my English class in school. That girlfriend at that time, has now been my wife for forty seven years.

The main thing I want readers to understand, is I am not writing this book for fun or to get attention, or for self gain. I have been very reluctant to write it at all and you will understand why after you read it. For several reasons I have not been led to write this book for twenty seven years after the episode itself. I am sixty-six years old now and as you read this book you will discover why I have waited so long to write it.

The reason I have chosen to write this book was really not a choice. I feel like it was God led. Approximately eight years after I had this bizarre experience, I woke up about three o'clock one morning from a sound sleep, literately sobbing with tears with the Holy Spirit speaking to me, telling me that I needed to write a book about my experience, possibly to help someone else that had faced a similar trauma in their life, to let them know there is help for them if they choose to seek God's leadership.

My experience was so bizarre and strange that it took me several years to sort out what was real and what was the fantasy world that I was living in, but I think I had to go through that experience for multiple reasons.

At the same time that the Holy Spirit was talking to me about writing a book, I had the impression from the Holy Spirit that it was not the right time to write it, I was to wait a while. I didn't understand that impression near as fully as I would learn over the next twenty years.

I am going to use real figures and data from my life. I pray that you will not look at my topics as bragging or being boastful. I feel like in order to demonstrate the power of God's blessings and his miracles in my life that it is necessary for me to use real information.

My hope and prayer by writing this book is to hopefully help someone else to understand a little better what might have happened to them from a similar experience, and I also wanted to let the medical field or psychiatrist hear about this experience from someone that has overcome it completely, and allow them to hear from a participant's perspective. I would even be willing to talk to the medical field or mental administrators about my experience if they so choose.

> The Lord is my shepherd;
> I shall not want.
> He makes me to lie down in green pastures;
> He leads me beside the still waters.
> He restores my soul;
> He leads me in the paths of righteousness For His name's sake.
> Yea, though I walk through the valley of the shadow of death, I will fear no evil;
> For You are with me; Your rod and Your staff, they comfort me.
> You prepare a table before me in the presence of my enemies;
> You anoint my head with oil
> My cup runs over.
> Surely goodness and mercy shall follow me All the days of my life;
> And I will dwell in the house of the Lord Forever.
> (PSALMS 23)

CHAPTER 1

The Beginning

We have all heard the saying to be careful of what you wish for, or for what you pray for. I am living proof that those words couldn't be spoken any wiser.

I had an experience earlier in my life that changed my life forever, and I believe it was because of my prayers such as that. There had been several instances with different people around where I lived, prior to my fortieth birthday, that made me begin to pray to God and ask why those people had such a strong testimony for what God had done for them, yet I was almost forty years old, had been raised in a Southern Baptist church since I was a child, and was saved by God's grace when I was thirteen years old, but without any extraordinary events.

When I was growing up I was very respectful of my parents, teachers, law enforcement, and authority. I never drank alcohol or used drugs. I am not bragging on myself, but I lead a very uneventful life, as far as anything bizarre, or super fantastic in the way of being a significant testimony of God bringing me back from a bad life, or bad habits. Most people looking on would call my younger years a pretty boring life.

My wife and I met when we were sixteen years old and she has always proclaimed that I have been an old man ever since she's known me. I actually take pride in her saying that.

I believe that any story should start at the beginning, therefore I have already gotten way ahead of myself; so let me go back to the beginning of my life and tell you the story that led up to this point.

I was born in 1952 and raised in a small farming community in south central Oklahoma in a town called Mannsville. My dad was a farmer, as well as my grandfather on my dad's side. My mother was a homemaker like most all other women were in those days. Very few women where I was raised worked outside the home. Most of them had a full time job cooking three meals a day, canning garden goods, washing clothes on a not so friendly old ringer washing machine or by hand, and raising kids. Most families had several kids, farm hands. Everyone seemed to want to grow their own farm help, was always my thinking. Either that or lack of birth control, or maybe those long winters nights without TV or any other entertainment might have been a contributing factor.

Most wives were farmer's wives and had kids from eighteen years old down to one hanging on one hip while she hung out clothes on the ole outside clothes line. We didn't have a clothes dryer through-out the years as I grew up. I don't know if there were any in the country at that time. Everyone had an outside clothes line to dry their wash. Momma had her washing machine in the back yard in a separate little building in my early childhood, and finally moved the washing machine into my brother's, and my bedroom. I remember momma washing out my little sisters cloth diapers by hand, and I never saw her use a pamper. I'm not sure if they even had throw-away diapers back then, but we didn't have money to buy them even if they were available. We actually didn't have an inside bathroom until I was about seven or eight years old. Most everyone back in those days had an outside toilet, called an outhouse.

Most people in my country when I was real young had
an outhouse, or outside toilet. Most farm homes didn't
have inside plumbing until I was a young kid.

I remember when my dad, along with my grandpa and an uncle, were digging our septic system for our first inside toilet. The hole for the septic tank was hand dug, by the way. The septic tank itself was built with hand mixed concrete and wire. I was missing school because I had a case of the mumps. I could see them digging the septic tank outside my bedroom window, so I would lay across my bed and watch them as they worked.

This is the back yard of the house that I grew up in. This picture
was taken in 1974 and it shows my dad's first cab tractor, (one
that had a cab on it). I bought this same tractor from him in
1978 as my first tractor. The little building in the back yard is
where my mother's washing machine was when I was young.

We were raised in what I call a box house. It had a kitchen and dining area in one room, a living room, and two bedrooms. My parents used one bedroom and my brothers and I shared the other bedroom. My oldest brother slept in one bed, and until he graduated from school and moved out, my middle brother and I shared the same bed. We also shared that room with the washing machine I spoke of earlier. The old house didn't have insulated walls, nor insulation in the attic when I was young. We had a sheet iron roof and I remember that it was the best sleeping atmosphere in the world, listening to the rain hit on the sheet iron. Later up in my teenage years daddy had insulation blown into the attic and it wasn't near as good to sleep by. It muffled the sound so you couldn't hear the rain hitting the sheet iron as well. We had only a pretty small propane heater in the living room, and a really small one in the bathroom, after daddy put a bathroom in. I remember momma would put flannel sheets on the beds every fall, and we used electric blankets as well. I remember how good those soft, flannel sheets felt back then. She would also put about three quilts on each bed and I would still almost freeze. They would be so heavy, once you got snuggled in you couldn't hardly move, but you didn't really want to move once you got your spot warm anyway. You would blow smoke from the cold air while lying in bed on a cold morning.

Most every piece of property in our country was farmed with either a row crop such as cotton, corn, peanuts, milo, or soybeans, or a small grain crop like wheat, rye, oats, or barley when I was growing up. There was always cattle raised on the country that was highly erodible, in low lying areas, or hilly property not suitable to farm, but farming was most people's livelihood during my early days.

As a small child life was very simple. No one in my community had much money, but didn't need a lot of money. Most people helped their neighbors harvest their crops and then they would turn about and help the other harvest theirs. Everyone grew a large garden for their food and the women and men together would harvest their gardens. The women would can everything they could because up until later on, as far I knew no one had a freezer around our home town.

I remember my dad telling a story when I was young that his brother, my uncle, borrowed $75 to make his entire crop on and struggled to pay it back. Most people were what we would call poor now days, but the funny thing about it is that everyone was poor so you didn't know any difference.

Meat was not very plentiful when I was young. I remember a neighbor would drive around with a freshly butchered hog iced down in the back of their truck trying to sell the neighbors a portion of it. They didn't have any way to freeze it, or keep it more than a few days. That was the way we obtained some of our meat. Everyone raised chickens though, and we had fresh chicken pretty often. My dad loved to quail hunt, squirrel hunt, and fish, so we were more fortunate than some because my dad was always bringing in fresh kill or catching a mess of fish. One thing I can attest to is that I never went hungry. My dad was a good provider and my mother was a wonderful cook. She could make anything taste good.

My younger years were pretty simple for me, but lots of hard work for anyone big enough to work in the daylight, then when it got dark most people went to bed early because with no TV and poor lighting there weren't many other options. Getting your work done before any playing, hunting, or fishing was the main emphasis with grown ups or kids either. Work was the most important thing before you could have any fun. My folks didn't even have a TV until I was fourteen years old, so I have seen many changes in my life as a small boy, from riding on a wagon pulled by mules or horses where my dad and his neighbors would pitchfork peanuts onto the wagon and haul them a ways down the road to where a stationary peanut thrasher was positioned for several of the neighbors to haul their peanuts to. My granddad had one of these thrashers positioned on his property. There, the peanuts were thrashed off the vines and the hay was sort of bundled into somewhat of a bale. Nothing like even the small square bales that came along later in my life that we still see today. I've seen that era of time, along with all the changes through time, up to all the modern conveniences and technology of today.

This was my grandfather's first and only tractor that he ever
owned. He farmed most of his life with a team of mules or horses.

My granddad had farmed with a team of mules, and retired
somewhere around the mid-1950s with a one row Allis Chalmer
tractor as his first and only tractor. My dad's first tractor was a small,
one row, A Farm-All tractor used to plow and maintain his crops.
When I was still under ten years old daddy had bought an H Farm-
All, then onto an International 300. When I was thirteen years old
daddy bought his first four row John Deere tractor, a 3020 series
in 1965. That was the tractor that I learned to run mostly, and I
still have that same tractor today. It still runs and functions properly.
Back then most farmers in my neck of the woods could scratch out
a living with a relatively small amount of acres to farm. There were
several farmers and sharecroppers in our areas. No one had many
acres to farm, because frankly they couldn't farm many acres with the
team of mules, or the small equipment they had. The funny thing
is looking back, all of those tractors in their perspective era were all
Cadillac's to the owners. Even the small one row tractors were the
best there was in that era of time. When a farmer got one of those he
was king of the hill until the next newest, bigger version came out.
Now those tractors look almost like toys. Life has many funny twists.

I remember as a teenager, even up in the mid sixty's, some men
still plowed their gardens with a team of horses or mules, but that
began to fade out as equipment become more prevalent.

My parents lived about three miles out of town and my grandpar-
ents on my mother's side lived in the little town that our community
surrounded, Mannsville, Oklahoma. My mother's dad was a carpenter

for the most part. He helped build houses and barracks for air bases and such. An hourly worker all his life, but that's the way most people still make their living today, punching a time card and working by the hour. It sounds strange to mention that, but there is an inside joke that I need to insert here. As a teenager my ambition in life was to become self employed by becoming a farmer-rancher and make my living without punching a time clock. I shut down the farming portion of my life when I was fifty years old, but I'm sixty six years old now and up to today I have still never punched a time clock. Not that I see anything wrong with punching a time clock, but it was just a kids dream to make a living and be your own boss. However, that only sounds good on paper, because someone, or something is always going to be your boss.

I have continued to raise cattle all these years, but farming cash crops like peanuts and corn stopped when I realized I wasn't making enough money to justify the amount of input cost and risk that it had become by 2002.

Since most people back in my early years didn't have TV's, most men in those days learned to play a musical instrument in order to entertain themselves during the long winter nights. My dad played a fiddle and mandolin and I had several uncles in the area who played guitars, banjos, and mandolin. Neighbors played steel guitars and other instruments as well. Most families that had several boys would actually have their own version of a musical band.

One of the best memories I have in those early days, is the neighbors would get together almost every weekend, and sometimes during the week, at night and sit out on the porch to play music together. Most everyone had a big porch in those days. Us kid's job during those festivals was to sit on top of an ice cream freezer while the men would crank the freezer until we had homemade ice cream. It was times like those that will leave you with memories that will last you for the rest of your life.

Several of the neighbors had rigged up a string of lights across their yard to light up the yard and the women and children would play croquette while the men sat on the porch and played music. Those were the days, as they say.

My young childhood was filled like most other young kids in those days, staying out of the grownups way, but we were always involved pretty directly with our parents in those days, and since there were no TVs, internet, or cell phones, families were a lot closer. For example I had two brothers and I was the youngest. My middle brother was two years older than me, while the oldest was five years older than me, but we were all required to be at the table for breakfast, lunch, and supper meals. Every meal throughout our growing up days, unless we were gone that particular day, we ate as a family. That's something that is seldom heard of anymore, and I think it would help our society today if that was still a requirement of all families.

This is my mom, dad, my siblings, and
I in 1962. I was ten years old.

When I was nine years old, my little sister was born and it wrecked my setup! I say that jokingly, but I was the baby of the family for nine years and I was extremely close to my mother. She actually spoiled all of us, but being the baby for nine years, I had a pretty good seat, if you know what I mean. Then along came my sister. Since she was the first and only girl, you can guess how my sweet seat got shifted pretty much out in the yard. I'm telling this as I laugh to myself. She'll get a kick out of this when she reads this book. Both my brothers and my sister are still living and doing well. We all live within fifteen miles of each other and still live in the area we grew up in. We still have family get-togethers around the holidays. The oldest brother is now almost seventy two. He and I travel a lot together, while my middle brother doesn't like to travel. He likes to be at home with his family. My little sister Martha, isn't so little anymore. She is now fifty seven. I'm just joking about my seat being shuffled out into the yard, because the one thing that my parents were not short on was love and affection. My mother was the most loving and compassionate person that anyone would ever ask for in a mother. On her death bed on January 1, 2012 as she lay in the hospital bed gasping for the last few breaths of her life, me and Lyndal, my middle brother, were standing beside the bed. Momma had a hospital wrist band on and I asked momma what she thought it said, she said, "I guess just my name." I told her no, that it said this is Vanilla Barnes the sweetest, most loving and compassionate mother in the world. She smiled and seemed to enjoy that. She was no longer breathing two hours later. She was eighty five years old. I wish everyone could have a mother like I had. She was the kindest, most loving person in the world and would do anything for anyone. She would sacrifice herself almost in any way for any of her kids or grandkids. Very rarely did I see her in a bad mood, down on life, or depressed. Only during the last five years of her life did she show the wear and tear of her health, and what life had done to her. She had a heart attack about five years prior to her death that almost destroyed her heart. Even with that, she fought and regained most of her capabilities back so she could take care of herself, and even through those later years she was still a fighter, smiling and trying to stay up beat.

This is my mom and dad as a young married
couple. Pretty dramatic difference in height.

One of the things that amused me was to see my parents together, Mother was every bit of five foot, two inches tall and my father stood six foot six inches tall. To me he was a giant not only in stature, but he was a very well respected member of the community. He was a very good farmer and took pride in everything he did. He was the kind of man that if he told you something, you could take it to the bank and expect it to be just that way. If he made a deal with anyone and shook their hand, it was as rock solid as a contract. He was a leader in the farming community in the area around us. He was instrumental in helping put together the organization to build a local farmer's co-op in our home town of about five hundred people so the farmers would have a place to process their peanuts, buy fertilizer, seed, and even feed. If there was a new model of peanut combine developed, he was one of the first farmers in our area to buy one. He was a leader and the other farmers respected him as such.

He was a man with lots of integrity and honesty, and he was hard working. His favorite motto when I was learning from him throughout my life was, "If it's worth doing, it's worth doing right."

If he built something, it was going to be straight, plum, square, and strong. He wanted it to be as good as he had the ability to build it, and he could build most anything he wanted to.

We didn't buy a lot of our equipment, we built it in the shop. We built peanut trailers, pipe trailers, cattle trailers, cattle squeeze chutes, and many other things.

If daddy bought a new piece of equipment, most of the time he would bring it home and make some kind of changes to improve it so it would fit his needs better.

My daddy was my mentor. From him, I learned how to build things, how to farm, and how to plow a straight row.

My dad could plow some of the straightest rows in the country. He taught me the art to do that as well. These are young peanuts that are about two weeks old.

He taught each of his children that it was important to take care of your credit and not to do anything to disgrace your family name, or yourself.

Almost everything that I know, I learned by working side by side with my dad. I'll cherish those memories for the rest of my life. He died when I was fifty two years old, and he is still my hero. He was eighty years old. He's been dead for fourteen years now and battled heart problems for fifteen years before death, but he, like my mother, kept moving and providing for himself up until his death.

When I hear the country song, sung by Arron Tippin, "You've got to stand for something or you'll fall for anything," I think of my dad. He had principals and integrity.

One thing that I can truly say that I am proud of, is that God showed his grace to both my mother and father by letting them stay active and mobile right up until their death. My grandmother on my mother's side was confined in a nursing home for approximately four years before her death. She first lost her hearing and couldn't communicate with us, then eventually lost her mind. She didn't know anyone. It was heartbreaking to go visit her and try to get her to recognize you. I prayed that my mother and father wouldn't have to go through that and God answered that prayer.

I started to add my mother and father, along with my wife, as I dedicated this book to both my wife and my parents, because they are the ones responsible for me being the way that I am, someone who stands for certain principals and ethics.

I'm not bragging on myself, but the ethics and integrity that my parents lived by was instilled in me and I live by those same principals every day. I'll carry them as long as I live. They are the back bone of my life and I am forever grateful to be raised by C. D. Barnes Jr. and Lovina Vanilla Barnes in Mannsville Oklahoma.

One thing that was actually kinda strange, and still causes me, along with all my siblings, to still wonder how our dad had such Aire around him. Meaning, he was never a loud person. I seldom heard him raise his voice, but when he told you to do something he was stern, but never mean, yet had all of our respect to the point that we wanted to please him. If you didn't mind him right away he would go outside in the yard and cut himself a keen switch off one of the Elm trees in our yard, then he would give you a whipping that you wouldn't forget. You didn't want many whippings from our daddy. We all four, still to this day, have the utmost respect for our dad and mother. We still also wonder how our daddy had such control over his family.

Daddy would preach and threaten us what he would do to us if he ever found out that we had drank any alcohol. As far as I know, none of us have drank anything in the way of alcohol, even at fifty-seven, sixty-six, sixty-eight, and seventy-one years old. When I was fresh out of school I had a friend insist that I take a taste of his mixed drink, or something like that, so I did taste of a few things, but I've never actually finished a drink, and as far as I know my siblings haven't either. It's still a mystery to all of us how daddy instilled that strong of a belief in each of us.

My dad would tell us that most all the people that he had known that drank a lot would waste their money and never save any for a rainy day. They normally weren't good managers because they would drink and party it up. I've watched that throughout my life and I have found that to be true myself. We believed daddy enough that we didn't want to take the chance of losing control of our management skills, or disgrace our family name. We all wanted to accomplish things in life and he taught us that you couldn't do that if you let alcohol get hold of your life. My siblings and I have all been somewhat good managers and I believe God has blessed each of us for keeping our nose clean.

As I grew and started to school, times were simple and slow, kids would play games around the school grounds. Back then the most popular games around the playgrounds were spin the bottle, kick the can, play mumble peg with your pocket knife, or play marbles. Marbles was probably the most popular for the boys. I actually don't remember how to play most of those games any more, but there were several simple games that people played just to fill the days and have some entertainment.

Some of the games were played on me. During my younger years and early teens we had a cousin that lived about half mile east of us. Back then we either walked everywhere as a kid, or rode a horse, or a bike. This cousin would walk across the pasture pretty often and play with Lyndal, my middle brother. Lyndal and him was the same age, so I was the young one and they let me know it most all the time. I wanted to play with them and sometimes they would agree, but sometimes they were mean to me. They would tie me up to the clothes line pole and go off down on the creek behind our house to play. They didn't want me along since I was younger. I would holler and scream until momma would hear me and come to the rescue.

She would untie me but the other two older boys had already left me behind and the ditch was pretty big, so I normally wouldn't try to go find them.

I remember the last whipping I got from my dad. Believe it or not I was actually deceived by this cousin and Lyndal. Now I will admit that I got away with things that I should have gotten a whipping for that I didn't, but nevertheless on this particular occasion mother had taken us to town and got us all a new water pistol. In the evening time daddy liked to sit out on the northeast corner of the house in the shade. That's where the house shaded the yard and back then there weren't very good air conditioners. Lyndal and this cousin and myself had made a game out of sneaking around the house and squirting daddy in the back with water with our new pistols. I had went around the house to the front door, went in the house to refill my water pistol with water. Daddy couldn't see who was squirting him but while I was gone the other two boys squirted daddy again and daddy told Lyndal and this cousin, "whoever is the next one to squirt me is going to get a whipping with an Elm switch." You guessed it, I didn't hear daddy say that so when I came out the front door the other two boys were waiting on me and dared me to go squirt daddy. Daddy cut one of those Elm switches and I got a good whipping and they got a good laugh.

My oldest brother Carl was always bullying over me and Lyndal. If we did something he didn't like he would slap the "fire" out of us. He was bad at slapping us for almost anything. Me and Lyndal decided he just liked to hit on us.

Daddy had a concrete block building that he used to store grain in. It had small windows up high on one of the walls used to scoop grain from a bobtail grain truck in through those windows. The windows were high enough that you couldn't reach them while standing on the ground, then it had walk in doors on other sides as well.

Carl always had hogs. He liked feeding hogs and raising pigs. So he had some milo stored in this building for feeding his hogs.

One day when this cousin was over, he and Lyndal locked me up in this building where the milo was stored, then they went around to those small windows and started throwing dried cow chips in through them trying to hit me. The results from that was that Lyndal and this cousin threw this trash into Carl's hog feed, and littered it up pretty bad.

Lyndal had started seeing a girl that lived down the road a ways, and he was in the bathroom cleaning up to go see her when Carl went to feed his hogs. He saw the mess that was left in his milo, so when he got back to the house he was mad.

Our bathroom was very small, just about big enough for two people to stand between the commode and the sink. The bathtub set almost against the commode on the back side from the door.

Lyndal was always big for his age and he actually had gotten about as big as Carl by this time, even though he was three years younger.

When Carl came into the bathroom and started yelling at us about what happened to his milo, I told him it was Lyndal and this cousin. Carl told Lyndal he was going to go clean it up before he went to see his girl, but Lyndal refused, and the fight was on. Carl started slapping Lyndal and Lyndal got mad and started using his fist and hitting Carl as hard as he could. He was tired of Carl's bullying and telling him what to do. I was in the bathtub hugging the back wall, trying to stay out of the line of fists flying while rooting Lyndal on, telling him to hit Carl hard. I was tired of Carl's bullying actions myself.

Our five foot, two inch mother came running into this tiny bathroom, trying to get between them and break up the fight. She finally got control of the situation. There were some red marks, and a few bumps on their faces. I personally was liking my front row seat. I hated to see it end so soon.

I guess Carl learned his lesson from Lyndal standing up for himself, because Carl never slapped either of us anymore.

Another funny thing is that I actually didn't want to be around Carl as we were growing up because he was mean to us, but after we got grown he and I have always been extremely close all through the years. We've traveled many miles together, hunted together on many different trips, and still plan trips together even today.

CHAPTER 2

Working Days

Most kids raised in our farming community were required to work as soon as you were able to hold up responsibilities, from simple chores as a small kid to helping plant the potatoes, onions, and other garden vegetables.

There will be a few terms that I will use throughout this book, one of them is graduation. When I was probably about eight years old I graduated into becoming a field hand. I was introduced to a hoe handle to help hoe the peanuts and chop the cotton.

Back then, there was no herbicides or chemicals to control weeds and grass in the crops. We generally hoed our crops about three times throughout the growing season to keep the crabgrass and other weeds from taking our crops over.

When I first started hoeing I was required to hoe only one row, while my middle brother hoed two. My oldest brother was old enough that he had graduated to where he hoed four rows at a time, along with the other grown-ups. As I grew I begin to hoe two rows, then graduated on up to hoeing four rows myself.

When I was about fourteen years old or so, herbicides started being used on a limited basis, and that started relieving us from hoeing so much. My oldest brother had left home by then, and I know he couldn't wait to leave home to get away from the farm because of the hoe handle. He said the farther he could get away from a hoe handle the better he would like it. He moved down in the Dallas/

Grand Prairie, Texas area for several years before moving back to our area to ranch cattle and work as a mechanic, then became Service Manager for our local John Deere dealer until retirement.

When I was about eight years old I was also introduced to a cotton sack, because back in those days everyone in the country raised cotton. There were several cotton gins in the area. When I started pulling cotton, momma sewed a shoulder strap onto a burlap sack. That was a small kids first cotton sack, then as you got bigger you graduated on up to a short cotton sack, then on up to a long cotton sack. A genuine cotton sack for a grownups was a long sock looking sack that was made out of canvas usually. The grownups pulled about a twelve-to-fourteen foot sack with a diameter of about thirty two inches or so. You drug it along behind you by a shoulder strap as you hand pulled the cotton boles off the stalk, and placed them into the cotton sack. When you would get to the end of the row or got your sack full of cotton, you would drag it to the trailer. Someone, usually the farmer that owned the field, would weigh your sack then record it down on a note book. Then you would dump it onto a cotton trailer and head back down another set of rows filling it up again. You got paid at the end of the job, or end of the week by how many pounds of cotton you had weighed in during that time period.

Grownups used canvas cotton sacks such as these, some
people in our country used even longer ones than these.

As I grew up into a teenager my cotton sack got bigger. I remember there was a local lady that I had the utmost respect for. She was a widow and was a working machine. I would try to pull boles beside her, but no one in the field could keep up with her. She would weigh in more pounds of cotton than any man in the field every day. She was a very sweet lady.

When I was nine years old my dad bought his first irrigation pump and several joints of aluminum irrigation pipe. Each joint was thirty feet long so it took two people, one on each end, to carry them or load them on a pipe trailer. There were seven joints of these pipes, which had screw gates on them to open and let water flow out and down the row. They called that type of irrigation, flood irrigation, where the water comes out of the pipe and then runs down between the rows of crop by gravity. You adjusted the amount of water that came out of each gate by how much you screwed it open. The gates were designed to open a little for a little water or a lot for more water.

That era of time was a lot of extra work that we had never been involved with before. We would unhook these seven joints of gated pipe, hook on seven main line pipe in their place, then go back and carry the seven joints of gated pipe down the turn row and re-hook them on to the end of the line. We carried these pipe by hand, one at a time for me and my middle brother since we were smaller, and two at a time for my oldest brother and daddy. We carried them several feet and then re-hooked them. We did this twice a day for the first few years.

This is my dad in our early years of irrigation. Notice the irrigation pipe at the end of the peanuts at the bottom of the picture. Also notice the heaviness of the peanut vines due to the irrigation water.

For the first few years of irrigation we camped on the river bank with the pumps to make sure that a problem didn't arise, such as blowing a line apart and getting our pump washed into the river. Daddy was extra cautious because it was all new to him. Those times had some good memories along with the hard work. We usually kept a trot line across the river and we would fish as we watched the pump. We had some good picnic time and family time as we stayed on the river as well as catching some fish to eat.

This is my middle brother, Lyndal, my dad and me
in 1967 hauling irrigation pipes to the field.

Some of our fields had to be leveled or reconstructed in order for this type of irrigation to work properly. Over the next few years daddy did some of this reconstruction himself by buying and using a land plane that he pulled behind his tractor to carry dirt, but he also hired construction companies to come in and move massive amounts of soil and reposition it in order for the water to flow properly.

Over the next several years, and as daddy would get another field level enough for the water to flow correctly, he bought more pipe and bought more gates. We would spend a lot of time in the winter months drilling holes and placing those gates into these blank pipes. That process was cheaper than buying pipes that already had the gates installed.

After several years of doing this we had finally placed enough of these gates in pipe, as well as daddy buying additional pipe so we could finally lay them all down in the early summer and leave them in place all summer long. After that we would only have to go to each field twice a day and open up about sixty five gates, then go back and close off the ones that had been open before as we would irrigate across a field. The pump only pumped a limited amount of water, so you had to only open up a certain amount of gates to match what the pump was able to pump. Each one of these "certain amount of gates," amounted to approximately sixty five gates and we called them "sets," so you might have twelve sets of water to irrigate a fifty acre field. Each set usually ran for twelve hours. Our normal time to change our sets would be about 7:00 a.m. and then again 7:00 p.m.

As I grew up and started my own farming operation I continued with this type of irrigation on my own cropland, along with buying Side Roll irrigation systems, as well as a pivot irrigation systems. I was involved with irrigating peanuts, Milo and corn from 1961 to 2002 when I quit farming those crops. I irrigate my Bermuda grass to produce hay for my cattle still today. Irrigation had been our life line to insure making a crop for forty one years. Over those forty one years there has never been a year that we didn't have to irrigate at least some. Some of the extremely dry years it seemed like we ran our irrigation systems almost continuously.

Prior to me graduating high school my dad and his brother owned a peanut digger and a peanut combine together, or thrasher, as some would call them, one of the first that was pulled by a tractor. The first pull-type peanut combines had a Wisconsin engine mounted onto the combine itself. The tractor was used to pull the combine, but the combine was self-contained. It got its power from the Wisconsin engine. Later on in life the engines were taken off and the newer combines, up til the present time, were PTO driven, powered from the tractor itself. My uncle ran the digger and dug the peanuts, then after letting them dry for several days, my dad ran the thrasher and thrashed the peanuts off the vines. In my later teens they had developed combines with overhead bins to hold bulk peanuts. We hauled our first bulk peanuts by bobtail trucks to Madill to be dried and processed. When I was sixteen years old my dad was instrumental in helping build the local peanut drying facilities that was our local co-op. From that point on my job was to transport the peanuts from the fields to the co-op.

This is a peanut thrasher that has a sacking platform up high. As you can see, there is a man bent over at the top of the thrasher as he works on the platform sacking peanuts. This platform was up higher on this combine so you could get a little breath of fresh air if the wind were right. My dad's first sacking thrasher was similar to this one, his next thrasher had a platform right down close to the ground where the dirt would just boil out of the side of the thrasher onto your head and shower you with dirt constantly. This thrasher was powered by the Wisconsin engine and the tractor was used to pull the thrasher. After sacking the peanuts on the thrasher, the sacks were then stacked by hand in the field, turned by hand every couple of days and dried for several days before loading them up by hand on a truck and hauling them to the processor.

During my older childhood and into my early teens the first mobile thrashers had a sacking platform on it where two people would stand, sack the peanuts, then sew the top of the sacks with twine, then dump it off the back of the thrasher. My uncle had a son that was about seven years older than me, so him, my two brothers, and myself were the sacking crew on the thrasher. Two of us would ride one round at a time. One of us would sack the peanuts under the spout while the other one would sew the end of the toe sack then dump it off the back of the thrasher. After we made a round we would switch places with the other two and they would do the same for a round. It was so dusty you could hardly breathe on the platform, so it was good to get some fresh air while the other two took their turn. We would try anything to breath, but the most effective thing we found to be most successful was to wrap a towel or cloth around your nose and mouth to filter the dust. By night time your nostrils and sinuses would be full of mud. That doesn't sound very pleasing, I know, but it's just the way we had to do things in the good old days.

During the peanuts sacking era it was very labor intensive. After the peanuts were sacked on the thrasher then dumped off on the ground, later we would have to go back and stand those sacks up on their end so the air could go through them for several days to prevent them from molding, we would go back and roll them over every couple days to help keep them drying. That was called field drying and it was necessary to prevent the peanuts from molding, souring or spoiling. After several days of this rolling and re-stacking we would then load the sack by hand onto a bobtail truck and haul them about fifteen miles to an adjacent town for processing.

My dad standing beside his first bulk combine that didn't require sacking. It has a big bulk talk on top for the peanuts to be blown into by a blower fan on the thrasher, then the tank would be hydraulically lifted, dumping the peanuts into a bobtail truck. The thrasher was still powered by the Wisconsin engine. This bulk process was a huge leap of progress in the industry to prevent so much hand labor with those sacks.

This is my dad's first thrasher powered by the PTO of the tractor. This is when the machines started being easier to maintain. It didn't have a separate engine to service and maintain.

When people talk about the good old days, everyone is referring to something different for each person. I have several mixed feelings about those days. The memories that I cherish the most is the people, like the lady in the cotton fields, how hard she worked and provided for her three kids she had at home. She never remarried after her husband got killed in 1961. She raised her kids by herself with nothing but hard work and determination. Those are the memories of the good old days that are special to me.

Almost everyone back then worked hard, that's all they knew. They knew if they were going to eat they had to work. Most work was just plain old physical farm work, or things such as plumbing, digging ditches, or carpentry in our country.

In 1966 my oldest brother Carl was drafted into the Army, and then after training was sent on to Vietnam. I was fourteen years old and that seemed to be when things got more serious, or grownup for me. My dad bought our first TV so he could watch the news reports on the Vietnam War. He was worried about whether my brother would ever make it home safely. Watching things on TV, like news about the War and worldly events became real to me for the first time. I could see the worry in my mother's and daddy's faces as they watched the news. Up until then I guess you would say things were out of sight out of mind for me.

Up until I was probably sixteen years old I made my spending money by pulling cotton for other farmers or by hoeing in other farmers' fields when I wasn't helping my daddy in his fields. As I got older in my teenage years I would take on day work and work for a local farmer for a few days between periods that my dad wasn't needing me. I worked with some by running tractors, plowing, and cultivating crops. I worked with one guy assembling Side Roll irrigation rigs together from the ground up, each one spanning 1,320 feet. I also worked building fences for neighbors.

This is me in 1967 shaking peanuts. Sometimes the peanuts
would have so much dirt on them that we would have to shake
them with this old converted peanut digger to help shake
the dirt off before they could be run through the thrasher.

Some of my elders around me today talk about the good old
days, but I for one am proud the mechanical cotton stripper was
invented and by the time I was in my late teens they began to start
showing up in our country. I was glad to see them. I am also very
thankful for the newer peanut combines that came along in the late
sixties. This new version had a bulk peanut hopper built onto them,
so we no longer had to sack the peanuts.

They can talk about the good old days all they want to, but I
got in on some of those good old days. I will forever be grateful for
herbicides and cotton pickers. I didn't like the end of that hoe handle
any better than my brother did, but the main difference is, that by
the time I was early in my teens herbicides came along and I didn't
have it as rough as either of my older brothers. There were a lot of
things about the good old days that were special to most people that
lived back then as well. For me, the most important thing that people
had back then was integrity. Back then most people were very hon-

est. You could trust what they said and everyone dealt by just a hand shake, they didn't need a contract.

When I was growing up we never locked our doors. In the summer time we had screen doors on our house. An old water swamp cooler was the only means of air conditioning. We slept with the wood doors open so the air could circulate through the house and usually lay in bed and still would sweat, but people didn't worry about getting robbed or your house getting broken into. Now days everything that you own has to be locked down or concreted in to keep someone from stealing it out of your yard. To me, one of the biggest changes in the years I've lived is the change in human character. You can't trust anyone anymore. Most people are after a free ride, or out to cheat someone out of something. Who would have thought about having to guard your identity, or your bank accounts from hackers. It is unbelievable to me how much people's behavior has changed in my lifetime.

I will say that I have had several friends over the years that still believed in the ethical way. Some of them have passed away. I've lost most of my close friends over the years, but I still have a few left. Most people like to surround themselves with likeminded people, but those kinds of people are getting fewer all along. I've had lots of friends over the years, people that I was raised around and also become acquainted with along the way. I've only had a few really close friends, ones you can depend on through the good times along with the hard times. One of our church members that has sold used cars for forty years made a statement the other day that I would agree with. He said when he first started selling cars forty years ago he felt like 90 percent of people were honest, but he said today he feels like 90 percent of people are dishonest. I believe he is making a pretty accurate assessment.

When I was in grade school I had begun to play basketball, which I fell in love with. I went to school so I could play basketball. Not really, but it was my favorite thing about school.

I was pretty much the biggest kid in my grade of about twelve kids, boys and girls, and that gave me an advantage in playing ball. I was pretty athletic and basketball was my game. I try to fool my grandkids into thinking that I was a good student, and I was an okay student. I made decent grades, but I struggled like most people. I had to really study to make good grades. I did take pride in trying to make good grades but my main focus was on basketball. I played from my grade school years up through my tenth grade year at Mannsville, and then in 1968 we lost our high school due to consolidation of school districts. I finished my last two years about six miles down the highway at a school called Dickson. I played basketball, but as a new-comer in a new school, I wasn't placed in the starting line up as a junior. I had to really work to earn a starting position my senior year because it was a much larger school with more players trying out for starting positions. I succeeded in becoming a starting player throughout my senior season.

After graduation in 1970 I began my personal farming career. I was farming peanuts and cotton the first few years of my life, but I was still feeling like a kid I guess and I loved to play basketball so much that I would find church leagues, independent leagues, or YMCA leagues to play at night after work up until I was probably twenty-six years old. The only reason I quit at that time was because I had been playing in a league that had run up into our planting season, when it was time to plant peanuts. We were playing the last tournament game to end the season when I came down on a man's foot and turned my ankle. I sprung it so bad that I tore all the ligaments in it. It swelled about twice its normal size and I laid up about a week with it propped up on pillows, throbbing with pain. Meanwhile, my brother and my dad had to plant my crops. I decided at that time, since I was self employed I couldn't keep being a kid any more, so I hung up my tennis shoes. Remember when I said earlier that I was raised that your work has to be done before you have any fun? I still live by those rules. I felt like a misfit laying up on those pillows in the house while my family members did my work.

There has been many memorable times in my life, but the most important one was when I was thirteen years old. We were having a revival at our church and the evangelist was Brother Honeycutt. I don't remember his full name, but nevertheless I was saved by God's saving grace during that revival and became a Christian at that time.

I have fallen short many times in my life of what a Christian should represent, but I can assure you that I have never lost my salvation. I have neighbors and friends that can attest to the fact that I haven't always lived truly like a Christian should, but in general I have never wavered from what I think are the main life lines of morality, honesty, and integrity.

I've talked a lot about my dad. He was not what you would call a Godly man in the sense that he didn't go to church all the time, nor did he lead his family in a daily devotion, and I never, til the day he died, ever heard him pray out loud. He was a leader of his family and tried to live a life that would be pleasing to God in everything that he taught us kids. He taught us that everything we did was a reflection on your entire family, that you never knew who was watching what you were doing and that everything you do, or don't do, does make a difference. He taught us that outward appearances are not always what they appear. It's what your made of and how you conduct yourself, that is the true story and that's what matters most. Daddy told us that he was saved when he was young, but was never baptized. Remember that comment, because later in the book that will become significant to remember.

My mother was a good Christian woman. She didn't hold daily devotions either, but she raised us in church and taught us about the Bible. She taught us how to conduct ourselves in a Christian like manner in everything we did in life.

I dated a few girls in high school, but never did consider myself to be a lover boy. I always wanted a relationship with a girl, so I usually had a steady girlfriend. The second most important time in my life was when I fell in love with a girl that has become my wife for forty seven years up to present, when I was sixteen years old. Her father was a Baptist preacher and he and his family, including my wife, moved into our community from West Texas to become our new pastor of our local Baptist Church, and since I attended our local Baptist Church, that's when I was introduced to Debbie.

I am very thankful to God that my mother raised me, my brothers and sister in church. I am also very thankful to God that he allowed me to meet my wife in church. A Christian girl that stood for principals and morals. My wife and I have talked many times how we both feel like God matched us up according to his will. I feel like he has a partner or spouse for each of us. We don't always look at it in that same sense when we're sixteen or eighteen years old. At that time most kids are just teenagers full of hormones, but it will usually show up before long, whether or not God puts you together, because marriage is not an easy task. My belief is that if God doesn't match you together it will be hard to ever stay together.

Let me tell the honest truth about me and my wife. We were pretty much totally opposites about our taste in colors and things when we first got married. If I liked something brown, she would want it in green, or if I liked blue she wanted purple. When we bought our first furniture, carpet, or whatever, it was a struggle because we didn't have similar taste. She has always liked antiques and I like modern, useable things. I am thankful that the longer we've lived together the more things we both like that are similar. The last Formica we picked out for our counter tops, we actually each picked the same sample, and likewise the last carpet we bought we agreed on as well.

We both like to argue a lot, so it wouldn't take much to get us into an argument. People around us would get tired of listening to us. I told you that to let you know that we haven't had a perfect marriage at all, far from it actually.

We basically had two things in common. We were both Christians and we were attracted to each other, so we fell in love, even with all the differences that we had between us. I've heard some people say they married someone with the same exact taste and had so much in common. That wasn't the case with us, so for us to live together for forty seven years has been a mystery for several of our friends. That in itself is a testament of the power of God. One of the key things that has held us together is the commitment we made to each other, and the commitment we made before God, actually stood for something. People say their vows today, but they fail to live up to the commitment many times. Commitment in a marriage is a rare thing anymore.

We both truly believe he placed us together for his plan. Her weakness is my strong suit, and my weakness is her strong suit. She is more of a nurturer and caretaker. She is a very compassionate person, where I am a planner and thinker about our financial well-being. She never worried about saving money. She has enough faith that God will take care of our needs. As for me, I feel like God gave me the mechanical skills and the mental capacity, along with the health, that he expects me to work hard to provide for my family and our future. Even as different as we are, we have made a pretty good team through it all, and we still argue a lot forty seven years later. We've come to realize, that is part of who we are, for good or for bad.

Just today as I'm writing on this book I was helping her earlier today hang some pictures of her great great-grandparents that she has never met. I made the comment that I like modern things on the wall to look at, people we actually know. Guess what? That started an argument, or let us say a difference of opinion.

Both my wife and I will tell you that if it had not been for our faith in God, sincerity in our wedding vows, and the belief in sanctity of home, we wouldn't have ever toughed it out because it has not been easy. There have been many trying times and hardships in our marriage.

We are all sinners just saved by God's grace. Even being a Christian I have had to fight several demons in my life and I'm sure my wife has as well. They come in many shapes and forms with different people, and many things that you didn't cause yourself and had no control over. They're brought on by other people sometimes, yet you get caught up into the effects or the circumstances, and it will tear your heart out or wreck your nerves.

My wife and I have both had many things thrown at us over the years that have damaged our nerves to the point that it's a wonder that we were able to pull it back together. We didn't overcome it by ourselves. God has a power and a sufficient grace that can repair things so it will be workable again if you will just seek his leadership.

If most people were honest I think that is part of life, and as a Christian that is how we grow. The obstacles in our path are tests and trials to let us see how powerful God is to see you through those times. It makes us stronger with a much more inspirational testimony.

Life has many different faces, shapes, hills, and curves to overcome throughout forty seven years of marriage. Today, most young married people thinks if things get tough, just abandon the marriage and try it again with someone else. That's not the way my Bible reads.

CHAPTER 3

Raising A Young Family

My girlfriend's father, J. D. Leavelle, had answered God's call to a church in Marion Indiana, so they moved the day after our high school graduation. We were not ready for marriage at that time, so Debbie moved with them. She got a job and began to work up in Indiana, and we were separated for about fifteen months.

After graduation I began going to a local college about sixteen miles away. The Vietnam War was going strong and several changes were going on in our society. I'm not going to go into particulars, because I've never been good with time frames or world events and such, but throughout my school days we saw the effects of DE-segregation in our schools, the Hippy Movement, people protesting the Vietnam War, President Kennedy, as well as his brother Robert Kennedy getting assassinated, and Martin Luther King. We also landed on the moon and experienced many different historical events that our kids are reading about in history books today.

About fifteen months after graduation, Debbie and I decided to get married, so on December 23, 1971, we were married.

My wife and I on our wedding day. December 23, 1971.

I had just harvested my first crop of peanuts and cotton. I was starting my farming career without much money, so I got a government FHA loan to help with operating the farm.

Throughout this book I will refer to stepping stones as I progress through life. I truly believe if you're trying to follow God's leadership, he has a purpose for your life. By him placing people and objects in your path he will lead you from one point of your life to the next. I refer to these as stepping stones of my life. He closes one door in front of you, and at the same time begins opening up another for you to step up to the next level, or phase of your progressive life.

The first stepping stone I will refer to is that I was able to rent a farm of decent size from a very nice local farmer who had retired shortly before. So I was blessed that opportunity came about just at the right time. I didn't realize it at the time but I know that was God's design. That property was very fertile and I was able to make a living for the first five years of marriage.

I know God had a hand in it because it was dry land farming, depending only on God to provide rain to help make a crop. Peanuts need lots of water to produce the best. That first five years of farming we had above average rainfall, therefore I was able to make above average crops for a dry land farm, because of extra rain.

After five years, the landlord sold his farm, which put me into a uncertain position of not knowing what was next, but God delivered the next stepping stone for me. He opened the door for me to rent two other small farms, small acreages, but one of them was a farm that I could irrigate the peanuts. Which in turn, allowed me to understand that it was meant to be. It was the first dry year of my young farming career. If I was still only farming dry land peanuts it would have almost been a failure, as far as making a crop. The irrigation produced a good crop and I was able to make enough to sustain a living.

At the time, I didn't realize what was happening, what God was doing in my life or my career. I didn't recognize it as such until later in my life, so I'm not going to mislead you into thinking that I was necessarily following God's directions. I was just trying to work hard to make a living. When you're young things just don't focus as well, or at least it didn't for me. I was eager and busy just trying to take the next move to help my little family survive another year. My belief is, and always has been, that if you work hard enough by doing things as good as you can, and for the right reason, God will bless it. I have always believed that hard work pays off, so my goal in life and my intentions at that stage of my life was to plant my crops with my very best ability, and I never doubted that I would harvest a good crop. I didn't say that I didn't worry about all the variations that came along, but truthfully I always had confidence in my work ethics.

God didn't make us all the same, thank goodness. This earth has to have all walks of life to keep it flourishing. Whether you're a plumber, electrician, farmer, or a preacher, we all have a purpose in life, and if God's hand is in your life, he will help you to progress throughout your life. He will place people and opportunities in your path to help along the way. Most times we don't even realize that it's God working through people to open the door for you, until later in life.

My wife, for the first four years of marriage, worked at a few different jobs to help pay some of the bills. Money was almost always scarce so we spent most of our time at home and my wife cooked most our meals that we ate. I was always catching fish, killing squirrels as well as deer, and we raised rabbits in our yard, so that was most of our meats. Our grocery bill was pretty cheap. We had couples invite us to go out and eat with them so we would go out with them a little right after our harvest season and when we had a little extra money, but most of the year we didn't have the money.

Throughout those years we had several young couples around us that were newlyweds as well and we would go to each other's houses and play cards or dominoes, and we played a lot of volleyball at church and just did simple things that didn't cost money.

I was beginning to get discouraged about my farming career and was about to give up on it and just go to work. We weren't farming enough to save much money and we lost another piece of property that we were farming, so I knew it was going to be hard to make a living.

We live in the Washita River bottom country. Almost one hundred years ago, a gentleman came into our country and bought up most of the good farming country around our home town. He wasn't willing to sell any of his land and it made it very difficult to expand your operation. Since money was tight I couldn't really afford to buy much land anyway.

When I was fifteen years old, I told my dad that I wanted to become a rancher and just raise cattle. He told me because of this family that owned most of the land around us, that it would be very difficult to lease enough land that I could count on for very long to make a living just ranching cattle, and I sure couldn't afford to buy enough. He told me that if I wanted to stay on the farm I would have to row crop and farm, because you can make more money farming than just ranching on a smaller amount of land. That's why I became a farmer. My passion was raising cattle and taking care of livestock.

As I was approaching the seventh year of my farming it was becoming more clear of what dad had told me when I was fifteen. I was having trouble keeping farms rented to make a living on. They were either being sold or someone would offer more money to lease than I could pay.

It had become a stressful time for my wife and I. I told my dad that if I couldn't buy a small farm, something I could count on having from year to year, that I was about ready to give up the farming life. My dad had bought a ninety acre farm about ten years earlier that I had been leasing from him. At this particular time, he was wanting to build a new house and needed some money himself, so he told me that he would sell me that ninety acres. I bought that property from my dad in 1977. He and my mother were able to build a new home, which gave them the opportunity to live in. The first and only new house of their entire life. I will add, it wasn't the kind of house that some might think. It was a 1,400 sq. ft, three bedroom home. Nothing fancy, but it was a castle to them from what they had always had to live in.

My dad and I had a very good arrangement between us. He told me when I started farming that if I would work for him and help him farm his farm and run his equipment like a hired hand and always be on the job, that he would let me use his equipment for the first few years of my farming career. That did two things; he had a farm hand to work for him without him having to pay a salary, plus I could use his equipment instead of having to buy a bunch of high dollar equipment myself. We kind of had a partnership, or a trade agreement, if you will. It benefited both of us in different ways, but didn't cost either of us much money. I bought my first tractor in 1978, then began buying plows and cultivators and such. I bought my first peanut combine in 1980, but I kept working along beside my dad even after I had started buying equipment. The arrangement we had between us still benefited both of us. We were each other's helpers. Neither of us had to hire help much.

We both had our own property. By then I had bought my own set of equipment and tractor, but we still farmed his and my farm as one unit. We would cultivate his peanuts and then go cultivate mine, or vice versa, with the same equipment. We both had similar tractors after 1978 so when we put a piece of equipment on a tractor, his or mine, we would use it on either of our crops as one unit. My dad and I had respect for each other, and went the extra mile to make sure we kept things fair. If he owed me money, he would pay it, and if I owed him money I would pay it. My dad told me that partnership between family members rarely worked, but we worked together intermingling our equipment and fuel for fifteen years. We never had but one misunderstanding that I remember, and that wasn't anything to do between me and him, it was a third party that was involved. We didn't agree about the way they were handling things.

One of the most important days of my life was when my oldest son was born. Leland was born August 16, 1975, which made me one of the happiest dads in the world. My wife had a miscarriage with our first baby in 1974, so we decided that she could stay home, and not go back to work while we tried to have a baby. It was a happy occasion when Leland was born, for more than one reason. It really tore my wife's world apart emotionally when she lost our first baby, and then having a perfect baby boy made her feel complete again.

I would like to insert something here, just because it fits this topic. When the movie came out recently called *Heaven Is for Real* was when the emotions hit me. Specifically in one scene of the movie where the little boy said he met his unborn sister in heaven. She didn't have a name because she died in her mother's tummy. That little girl was a growing child in heaven. That was the first time in my life that reality actually became real, that I would get to meet my unborn baby that we lost in 1974 in heaven someday due to my wife's miscarriage. I sobbed with tears. The reality hit me so hard, I am crying as I'm writing about that experience right now.

After Leland was born, Debbie went back to work. She and I both began to pray that God would open up an opportunity of some kind to give us enough farm land to be able to make a good living, without Debbie having to work outside the home. My desire was for her to be only a homemaker and raise our family. I didn't want to be burdened to have to leave the kids at day care.

The next major stepping stone that God had planned for us happened in 1978, when my uncle retired and called me to ask if I would be interested in renting his farm. That was the prayer that Debbie and I had been praying for. It would give us enough land after a couple years of recovering from the initial investment so she could quit work. The agreement that my uncle wanted to make, was that I would rent his farm for a few years and then he would consider selling the land to me. His farm was one hundred acres of prime irrigated peanut land, some of the best soil type in our area for raising peanuts.

On July 25, 1980, our second son was born, Nathan, which also was one of the happiest days of my life. He was another of God's perfect little miracles that had all his right parts in all the right places. At that time, Debbie and I felt like God had allowed us the opportunity to acquire enough land that she wouldn't have to go to work outside the home, so from then on her job was mainly focused on raising kids, cooking, cleaning house, and her and my mother did a lot of canning garden vegetables. Farm wife life. It's still hard work.

A big setback happened in 1980. We suffered the worst drought that I suffered at any other time in my thirty two years of farming. That summer started off in the spring extremely dry. We had to lay most of our irrigation pipe and actually irrigate dry beds of our fields just to obtain enough moisture to plant, then we had to pick up all the pipe, let it dry a few days, and start planting. We had to do a lots of double work in very extreme heat. The summer months were so hot that year that the peanuts grew the largest vines of any other year, but we couldn't get enough water on them to set the pods. In other words, couldn't make the peanuts produce on the vine. As it drew toward fall, I had a disastrous crop and huge vines, but the pods had just started setting on the vine late in the fall when it actually started cooling down some. There wasn't enough time for them to mature into a good quality peanut. Everyone in the country had a short yield that year and with most farmer's crop setting their pods late, they were sorry quality along with weak yields. I thought I was going to have trouble even paying my FHA notes that year. It would be almost disastrous, but then God stepped into the rescue. All the peanut Sheller's who normally bought our peanuts started anticipating a shortage of peanuts themselves, so they started offering a big bonus on the peanuts for any of the peanuts we could actually get to the market place. Along with that, my dad and I baled thirteen thousand bales of peanut hay that year, because of the huge vines, more hay than we'd ever produced before, or since, and we were able to sell that hay for a top price. When the dust settled with all the added features that year, the bonus money, along with the sale of extra peanut hay, that disastrous crop turned into a normal amount of income for me, and my dad.

Over most of my life it seemed to work like that. No matter how bad my situation looked at some point, God always seemed to help out in some way to make it more bearable. I had weaker crops than others, but I can tell you that I never had what I would call a disastrous crop that wasn't offset by God's help like he did in 1980.

I have had many different circumstances on other things, besides crops, that looked very bleak, but through different chains of events, it never came out as bad as it appeared. Some were still not good, necessarily I'm not saying God will ease all your burden, but someway God would make it better than it originally appeared. God's grace would always show through in some way.

To finalize my uncles land deal, in 1982 we were able to buy his land to complete God's plan and my uncle made it affordable. He wanted a down payment and let us make payments to him and his wife for ten years. He set up the payments so it wasn't too over-whelming. I know God had a hand in that transaction because we were still struggling with money and that was the only way we could have made it work. I feel sure that God laid that kind of configura-tion on my uncles heart for two reasons. One, so we could make it work for our budget, and it also helped my uncle because he wasn't taxed as much because he took it in payments. God has a way of working things out. Sometimes you can't see what he's doing at the time, but if you'll look behind you he's been there making things happen for a reason.

We finally knew we could count on that farm to be something consistent that gave us enough land to allow Debbie to stay home for twenty years so she could raise our boys and help me any way I needed help.

One of the best memories during those years was when we would be thrashing peanuts in the fall. My wife and my mother would prepare sandwiches and they would bring them, along with my kids, to the field about supper time and we would have a little family picnic supper in the field and dad and I would get to enjoy visiting with the women and playing with the kids for a few minutes before we fired up the combines again. Little things like that has left good memories to look back on, simple things.

My sons Leland and Nathan as youngsters.

My young family portrait in 1981.

Debbie was, and still is a dedicated hand. Whatever I needed help with she was a willing hand. Some of it she volunteered for, and I think she probably regretted when she got into it, but she never backed up or refused to help.

I was the kind of person that I would do several different little things other than just farm crops in order to make ends meet. We were still just surviving. We never had a lot of extra money, but I had got to looking at the corn prices along in our early years when our boys were too young to work much, and the corn prices were cheap. I also looked at the price of fattened hogs and they were a respectful price, so I told Debbie I'm going to feed out some hogs. She told me that I was on my own when it come to the hogs, she wasn't messing with any hogs.

I had a neighbor that had been feeding some hogs and had quit, so he had some hog panels and feeders not in use and told me that I could borrow them. I went and loaded them up and since I didn't have any help to put up all those panels, Debbie was gracious enough to show up down there and help me. We made enough money that first year that I bought those panels off my neighbor, and bought some more hogs. The second year, Debbie also told me she wasn't helping that year. It wasn't long after that when I started buying young pigs and needed someone to hold them down while I castrated them, guess who was holding them down for me? Yes, it was her. That's when you know you have a dedicated wife.

My wife and sons bottle feeding baby calves. In the background is my first peanut thrasher.

My middle brother Lyndal and his wife were bottle feeding baby calves so we also started bottle feeding baby calves in those early years to make extra money. We would buy baby dairy calves from local dairies and Lyndal and I built some calf sheds and pens to hold them separately. I put up a little barn and put hot water in it so we could wash the bottles out. My wife and I have had as many as fifty two calves on bottles at the same time. We raised a few hundred calves for the next few years. Debbie was the main bottle feeder for the calves. When I told you earlier that God places couples together for better or worse, he gave me a good help mate. She has been through the thick and thin, the clean and nasty, right along beside me. We have done several things on our farm other than raising field crops in order to survive, but with God's help and guidance we've been successful.

My dad retired in 1986 and started fishing. He put as much passion, effort, and dedication into his fishing as he did his work. He started making his own catfish punch bait, and when he would go to the lake and catch fish, sitting beside other fishermen who weren't catching fish, he would sell them a bucket of bait. Before long he had steady customers buying C. D.'s Catfish Bait. He built up a pretty good business in his back yard making bait and selling it. Now don't get confused, he used about as much as he sold. He would furnish enough catfish to feed our whole church a few times per year.

Like I have said earlier in this book, if my dad did anything, he wanted to be the best he could be and do as good a job as could be done. He studied and planned how to make a better bait all along. His clientele showed how well he was doing when he passed away. Daddy had about thirty five, five gallon buckets of bait partially mixed up when he went to the hospital his final trip. My nephew helped my mother finish the mixture so she could sell it. Several people wanted his recipe after his death.

I feel very fortunate to have worked with my dad side by side for fifteen years as an adult before he retired. After my dad retired he kept his tractor and peanut combine and he would help me run tractors, and I would pay him by the hour when he worked. I also leased his farm, which along with my own, doubled my work load.

Dad wasn't interested in working a lot of hours, so in 1989 I decided I needed a full time hired hand. Daddy sold me his tractor, combine, and the rest of his equipment, and I hired a full time helper.

As our boys grew, they would help around the farm by hoeing and running tractors, laying irrigation pipe, or whatever I needed help with, but by the time the oldest one became a teenager I had hired this full time hand, so between me and the hired help, we did most of the tractor work, although my sons got in on plenty of tractor work as well. Our boys weren't required to work near as hard as I had to as a teenager. That is also a sign of the progression of time. There were more modern herbicides and chemicals that helped us all. I'm sure when they read this book they may disagree because they still got in on enough and made good hands, but it wasn't too steady. What they did get in on was some of the hardest work we had to do though, laying those irrigation pipe every summer and picking them up every fall wasn't easy work.

I don't believe that working hard and teaching your kids to work hard ever hurt anyone. I think that is what God expects us to do. Today people seem to be afraid they're going to hurt their kids feeling to ask them to help. I won't ever understand that. The Bible speaks about working by the sweat of your brow.

I worked my boys pretty hard at times, but I never abused them, and if they told the truth today, I hope they would tell you that I taught them that hard work is the only way that you can survive in this world.

Second Thessalonians 3:10 says, "For even when we were with you, we gave you this rule: If a man will not work, he shall not eat."

For years my wife and my boys called me a workaholic, and rightfully so. By the time they were in high school, it seemed like there was never enough time in the day. The government was changing the laws on the farm. They were signing new farm bills that were taking our profit away, so I was adding other facets to our operation to try to stay ahead of the losses we were suffering until I was neglecting my family time. All I seemed to do was work, because I didn't see I had a choice.

My biggest regret in my life, was that I got so busy during the critical times of my son's lives that I couldn't spend much time with them, and that goes back to my belief that your work had to be done before any play time. I had gotten to the point that I could never catch up on my work, so I didn't have time for any play time.

One of the worse things about that period of my life is when I had as much stress on me as I did. I know that I was short tempered, hateful, and snappy to my wife and kids. I can never take back those years, nor my actions, and that is something that will haunt me until I die. To my family members, I'd like to say I'm very sorry for my actions during those years. They all caught my wrath. I was never physically mean, nor did I use brutal tactics. I've never laid an angry hand on my wife, but they will all tell you that I can cut you like a knife verbally.

Leland with one of his first deer kills.

Nathan with his biggest deer to date. He killed
him when he was only about 15 years old.

Leland with his biggest deer to date and me with a nice buck.
Eating what we killed was a large part of our survival. Most
everything that we hunted and killed was cleaned and eaten.

From the time kids are big enough to play, up until eighteen
years old, they want to have fun and do things that are fun, but I
was so stressed trying to keep things afloat that I didn't have time

for much fun, especially in the summer months. After harvest in the fall I would always take them deer hunting, which I think was one of our most favorite things to do as father and son, and they both became good hunters. I had hunted for several years prior to them starting to hunt, had logged many hours in the woods, put up deer stands and such, then I would take them as young teenagers and put them up in my old deer stands. The funny thing about their young hunting careers is they have both killed bigger deer in their first few years of hunting than I have ever killed up to this present time, and they killed them out of my own deer stands. I would tease them about putting it on their old man, or I would aggravate them and try to take part of the credit for their success since they were hunting in my stands, but I wouldn't have it any other way. I was proud of their accomplishments.

I would also try to make up part of my neglectfulness during the summer months by spending the winter months hauling my boys to livestock shows. We all enjoyed showing hogs. That was our main family time while they were teenagers.

We started buying a few hogs for Leland when he got old enough, and then we decided to start raising our own hogs. Myself, along with the hired hand, built three insulated farrowing barns in my shop with fans in them. Really nice ones. Each one held four sows at a time while birthing babies. Guess who was the main care taker of those baby pigs for their first six weeks of life? Yes, Debbie, my wife. Whatever was the requirement, she stepped up to the plate. I will say though, as our hog operation grew into several sows and pigs she didn't continue with those chores. They were mostly done by me, the boys, and the hired help. This all started about 1988 or 1989. That was the beginning of one of the roughest periods of my life, as well as the busiest periods of my life.

My wife with our first litter of raising show pigs and it grew
from there. It took the whole family. My wife with the pigs
and my sons made good hands with the hogs and cattle alike.

In 1989 I repeated what my daddy had done twenty years earlier. I was instrumental in forming a corporation to buy the old peanut co-op back so we would have a place to process our peanuts.
The local peanut co-op had gone broke several years earlier, and new
owners had bought it and ran it for a few years. At this time they were
going bankrupt, so I gathered seven other local peanut farmers, along
with myself and my brother in law. He had just moved into our area
and he was a CPA. Because of his knowledge and understanding of
corporate laws I talked him into joining us farmers, and we formed
a corporation. My sister-in-law came up with the name, "Mannsville
Agricultural Center," and we began that business, as well as me keeping up with the other things I had going. If that facility had closed
down for good the farmers would have had to haul their peanuts
several miles away to be processed.

The next stepping stone from God was also in 1989. This is a
true testament of what God can do. There were eighty acres of prime
farm land that lay west of my home, beginning within one hundred
feet of the back door of my house. That eighty acres would be a huge
addition to our little family farm. It was adjacent to our original

ninety acres that we had bought in 1977, and that was where we had built our little FHA house. I had tried to buy it ten years earlier. I found out at that time, it was in an estate and the people that owned it lived in another state. I didn't have anyone's phone number so I went to the local court house and got a name and address and wrote them a letter. The executor of the estate wrote me back and told me it could never be sold because of the way it was set up in the estate.

In 1989, something told me that I needed to check on that property again, and it wasn't a person that told me, I just had a feeling come over me for no apparent reason. I didn't have the guy's phone number and had long since lost the address I had written down ten years earlier, so I went back to the court house and got the name and address and wrote the executor a letter, asking if I could lease the property since I knew it couldn't be bought. A couple weeks later I received a letter back from this man. He told me that there had been some changes made in the estate, and the owner had passed away. He asked me what I would pay for the land if I was still interested in it. I wrote him back and told him I was definitely interested, but I would prefer to talk to him by phone if he would send me his phone number. A few weeks later I got a letter with his phone number.

I called this man and he told me that the situation on the property had changed and that it would eventually be sold. There had to be a probate and such, but he asked again, what would I pay for it? I asked him who all would bid on the property. My heart sank when he told me that the family that I told you about earlier, who owned most of this country around here would also have an opportunity to bid on it. I told him what I would offer for an opening bid. I also told him that if I had to I would probably pay a little more if he would be kind enough to give me a second bid, but I also told him that there was no way that I could stand toe to toe with that other family and outbid them. I didn't have the money that the other party had.

Believe this or not, I had never met this man, and until this day I've never met him yet, and why he replied how he did is nothing short of God's hand at work. His reply was this, "you won't have to stand toe to toe with that family. I feel like I'm obligated to give them a chance to buy it, but I know them well enough to know they will bid it cheap, but I promise you that I will give you a second chance before we sell." I told him that was fair enough.

Almost a year passed, I'm thinking they have already sold the land to this other party but I thought I'd call him anyway. To my amazement, they had been waiting on the probate and legal affairs. He told me that the other party had given him a bid, told me what he thought it would take to buy it, and ask if I would be willing to pay that. I told him what I'd pay and we made the agreement on the phone. He told me to get my attorney to fix up a contract and get the ball started. Two months later, my attorney had the papers ready. He sent them to the sellers and they signed them, and my wife and I signed our side of it, and we became the owners of the land that I tried to buy ten years earlier. I have still never met this executor, but I can assure you he has integrity and honor, and he earned my respect throughout that ordeal.

There is no doubt that God arranged that, from giving me the impression that I needed to check on that property at that precise time, after being told ten years earlier that it could never be sold. Totally out of the blue that came upon me, then the executor being so nice to work with me to allow me the final bid, and opportunity to purchase it. It brings tears to my eyes as I'm telling this story because of the miraculous way that it all came about. We needed that property so badly and I know it was divine intervention that gave us the opportunity, no doubt.

That year was also the beginning of several other events. I sold all of my cows that year to raise enough money to buy the eighty acres of land, so I started rebuilding a cow herd. I actually bought several registered Angus cows and heifers, and over the next several years bought more cows, and ended up with about 150 mother cows. Several of them were registered, with the responsibilities of tattooing baby calves, filling out forms on each calf to register them. My sons were a big help on the cattle. Helping tattoo babies and working cattle. Both boys are good cowboys. They enjoy working with livestock much more than farming.

We had also started raising baby pigs. We ended up over the next few years building boar barns, and sow pens, and built a very nice hog feeding floor for our show pigs and sows.

Leland showing one of his good pigs in the
show ring while in high school.

I had help from our local county agent. He was a very good "hog" man. He was very knowledgeable about blood lines, sows, and boars. I will give him the credit for our success as far as our breeding program.

He helped us buy sows and breed to certain boars, and in the first season of raising pigs we raised and sold the breed champion at the Oklahoma City Junior Livestock Show, which is one of the biggest shows in the country. There were usually about three thousand barrows of all breeds showing at that show. In other words, if you had a breed champion at that show you really were making a statement about your breeding program. That fall we raised and sold the reserve Grand Champion at the Tulsa state fair, another prestigious show. With that kind of success came recognition from several good feeders, not only in Oklahoma, but also buyers were coming out of Texas and New Mexico. Another credit to our county agent for knowing so many good feeders and him getting them to come and look at our pigs.

Nathan showing one of the Duroc gilts that we raised.

Over the next ten years we grew our hog operation up to thirty eight brood sows, and four clean up boars. We artificially bred most of our sows, but nonetheless we had a lot going on. We had the sows, along with the 150 mother cows, as well as farming about 350 acres of irrigated peanuts and corn. Now a days that wouldn't be considered a very large farm, but back then, with minimal help, it was a load along with all the other things going on.

It isn't hard to figure why my family would call me a workaholic, or figure why I didn't have time to play or go on trips, or have fun. I just hope they have forgiven me, because I really didn't know anything else to do back then but just keep growing our business bigger and working hard, trying to replace some of the money we were losing from the changes in our farm bills.

Leland and Nathan. These two young cowboys made
good hands with the cattle and hog operation as well
as farm hands. It took all of us to make it work.

Early in our marriage, Debbie didn't like not being able to plan things. On the farm you have to be on twenty four hour call. Something was needing attention all the time, many times without warning. It would just happen suddenly. If the cows broke down the fence, or the river started to rise, I had to keep a very close eye on it to keep it from sweeping away our irrigation pumps, so early on we adopted a standard that we still live by today. She would plan on going on vacations and trips with her parents, or she and her sisters would take the kids on trips in the summer while they were out of school, and I would take my vacation after harvest time when I wasn't needed as badly on the farm. That seemed to work pretty good, because like I stated earlier in this book, we have such different taste in even what we enjoy doing on vacation.

That has really worked out for the best. I would usually go on an out of state deer or elk hunting trip, which she would have no interest in, and she could take the kids to a theme park or some historical museum, or whatever. Because of me having irrigation pumps sitting along the river bank all summer, and knowing how fast the river could come on a raging rise, I couldn't leave home in the summer months while the kids were out of school. Plus I was changing irrigation sets twice a day trying to make the best crops I could.

Even later on, after the kids are grown and I no longer have pumps sitting on the river bank, we still follow about the same pattern. She enjoys going on trips with her sisters, and I like to go on hunting trips with my oldest brother and our oldest son. As he became an adult my youngest son is not into hunting as much as the older one is.

These two handsome men are my sons as grownups. They clean up pretty good for a couple of farm hands, don't they?

CHAPTER 4

My 90-Day Journey With The Devil

For me to set the stage for this chapter, I need to take you back several years and tell the events that led up to this point in my life. To continue with some of the first comments in this book, there were several things that happened in my life in the 1970s and 1980s that set the stage for the events that took place in this chapter.

Ever since I was a young child, I had attended church. Not to brag, but I was a pretty good kid who didn't drink alcohol, go to night clubs, or much of anything that I felt would disrespect my parents or myself, as I said earlier in this book. I had led a pretty quiet and boring life, as far as other kids.

Sometime during those two decades, we had a guy come to our church named Yo Yo Collins. He was crippled and restricted to a wheelchair. His testimony of how he had been injured and wound up in that condition really inspired me. His accident almost ended his life, but yet through Gods help and grace, he fought back, regained enough mobility to a limited functionality, then he became a gospel singer. His testimony of what God had done for him and through him really touched my heart.

In 1978 two men escaped from the McAlester prison and went on a thirty four day killing spree around the surrounding towns where I live, killing several people, including several law officers. At one point in their path, they were held up in a farmers house about forty miles east of my home where they tied up the farmer, stole his truck, but let him live because that particular farmer had let one of the inmates hunt on his land in prior years. Letting him live was a miracle in itself. Very few people that came in contact with these two men over the past thirty four days while they were, "at large," were left alive. They killed eight people, including three law officers over that thirty four days. That farmer later came to our church and gave his testimony of the experience, and I again was inspired by that man, giving God the glory of letting him escape harm.

Later on, probably in the 80's, a highway patrolman, by the name of Rocky, had made a traffic stop that ended up in a gun battle in which he got shot and wounded. I don't remember his last name, but it happened pretty close to my home town. Later, he came to our church and told of his experience. He gave God the glory for delivering him from that terrible situation that day.

After each of these magnificent testimonies would happen I would pray to God, "Why don't I have a powerful testimony?" I've been raised in church, been a good boy all my life. I really don't have anything too appealing to tell about what God has done for me except save my soul when I was a teenager. I would pray to God something like, "It would be good to have a horrific testimony, one that would make a major impact as I told it, or inspire people like I was inspired each time I heard one of these men." Little did I know what I was praying for.

The next step to set the stage of where I was in my life was one of the most devastating things that happened pertaining to my farming career, it happened in 1989.

The government signed into law the NAFTA Trade Agreement which was to try to put the US commodities and farm products on the same price levels with all other countries, even though their input cost was much lower than ours. I'm not smart enough to tell you all the details about the program but from what I read and was able to understand about it, it would be detrimental to our small family farm, along with hundreds more family owned farms.

When I heard they had signed that agreement into law, I told my wife, "that agreement will force us out of farming." I told her in 1989, that it might take ten years to cause us to go broke, but it would happen. We needed to start looking for other ways to make a living. I was a third generation farmer, and to some people's surprise I'm sure, I was very proud to be a farmer. I took pride in being the best farmer I could be and I know it wasn't a glamorous job to most people, but I felt like it was my calling. I fully intended to retire a peanut farmer like my dad and my grandfather had.

The next few years became very depressing for me. I worried about what I would do. My life's ambition was to stay on the farm and continue some kind of living through the farm life. I know now, by looking back, that I was miserable. I was so burdened by stress that I made life tough for my kids and my wife. I said things and did things that I will always regret, and I hope they forgive me. That was really no excuse, but I was so consumed about going broke, that's all I could think about, and I made everyone around me reap my wrath.

My wife has a sister and brother-in-law in Illinois where we'd visited over the years, and I'd met some of the local farmers around their home town. Many of those farmers farmed their fields and grew crops, as well as having a large hog raising facility or fed cattle in confinements as well. We traveled back to Illinois, where I re-visited several of their facilities to see if I could make something like that fit my farming operation. More in the way of feeding animals rather than row crops. Every operation in Illinois I looked at had potential, but the down fall was, they would all take a lot more money to get any one of them up and running, and we still owed quite a bit of money on our farming operation at home from farm loans, so I wondered how would I ever make my payments. I would have to borrow a lot more money to get any one of them implemented on my farm in Oklahoma.

For the next couple of years I was still fighting depression and looking for anything that would help make a living, when I was introduced to a multilevel marketing scheme that blew my mind at that time.

I'm sure I'm not going to tell this part like some people would see things, but in the spring of 1992 computers were pretty new to me. This program I was introduced to, was a membership to go on the computer where you could buy about anything in the world on the internet and have it sent to your home. The company structure was for you to sell memberships into this program where they would be set up in a pyramid system so that everyone you entered into the system you would benefit a percentage of what they bought, as well as the people they would get to join. In turn, you would also benefit from what they bought.

In my mind, this was a similar program such as Amazon is today, but this again was 1992, long before Amazon, and each person that joined had the potential to benefit money from all the down line that you, and the people that you got to join, also got to join. I have always been good in math and figuring things, and looking back on it today, I still see the mathematical possibilities of how anyone could potentially do very well. When their propaganda was presented to me, with me being in a very weak state of my life and hungry for anything to keep from going broke, it hit me, like this was my answer. This had tremendous mathematical possibilities to become pretty wealthy, and save our livelihood.

I joined into the pyramid, bought their literature, and started trying to recruit new memberships. I got very serious about it in a hurry, and it began to consume my life. I was going to multiple meetings a week, setting up meetings of my own, and trying to recruit members of my own. I began reaching out to people that I thought needed extra income, and if they couldn't afford to pay their entry fees to become a member I would pay for their memberships myself. To say I was excited about this new found business was an understatement. I was engorged with enthusiasm, mainly because of the income I was expecting to come from this pyramid.

I got so involved to the point that I wasn't sleeping at night, I was roaming all around, which made my wife unhappy. When I was at home, all we were doing was arguing. I began neglecting my farm and the things I should have been doing there.

I did have a good hired hand, and I'd touch base with him and kept him things to do, but I looked at this new business as my salvation, my new life line. My daddy always thought that they brain washed me. I've always heard that phrase, but never really understood the true meaning, but I have a different explanation that I'll share later on.

From this point on in this chapter, I ask for your forgiveness up front. I will try to explain what I think happened to me. I will tell you the honest truth of what I think, but after all these years, many hours in prayer about it, and still not being able to find the absolute truth, I cannot know for sure myself, so I can't possibly expect the readers to understand it. I will only ask you to read it and try to understand it as best you can, and hopefully someone that has experienced anything similar might can benefit from my experience.

Over the next few weeks I had gotten acquainted with a lady that seemed interested in helping with my plight. Since my wife wasn't understanding my enthusiasm for my new business very well, I made arrangements to keep some of my material at her house.

A lady that I knew vaguely, seeing that I was in a vulnerable state of mind, asked me one day while I was sitting in a chair in her house, if I would like to feel better than I ever had before. I naturally said yes. She said some kind of ritual and something felt like it came into my body, just a warm, relaxing feeling where I just laid back in that chair and almost went completely limp with such a relaxed, pleasant feeling. From that moment on, I began to feel like something inside of me was telling me where to go and what to do. My determination to keep building this business got even stronger.

When I would come home, my wife and I would get into arguments. She began to beg me to get out of that business, and she would tell me that I had something wrong with me. I would tell her that she was crazy. My neglect for my family and my farm was getting worse.

I was running in all directions, and wasn't sleeping much at all. I'd tell my wife I was going in one direction to a certain town, but when I pulled out of the driveway this power inside me would tell me to go the opposite direction. I literally believe that I was being driven by some kind of super power, like I didn't have control over my body. I was being controlled by something else.

It was the time of the year when we took our boys and their hogs to the Oklahoma City Junior Livestock show each year.

During the time spent in Oklahoma City, which was probably five days, there were several things that happened that I can't explain. My family, along with some of our friends, would go into a store and I would start talking to a stranger, but I would seem to know a lot about them. I remember going into a McDonald's talking to an airplane pilot. I knew more about him than I should have. When we were in our motel room a young lady named Sara called our room, and she and I talked as though we knew each other well. We also got to talking about scriptures. It was very strange to me, as well as my wife and friends.

My youngest son was eleven years old at that time. I remember wanting to go across town and look at some stock trailers while we were waiting to show the next hogs some time later. I was shopping for another cattle trailer. He wanted to go with me, so when we got to the trailer dealership, I met a young lady that I knew from back home that would eventually become one of the two young ladies that I became infatuated with. She was working there and we talked a while, looked at several trailers, then when we got back in my truck, this power within me directed me to turn down a certain road out in the country and we drove for probably fifteen miles. We were out in the country along some wheat fields that I never knew existed. My son kept asking me where we were going, and I'd reply that I was just going for a ride. I believed at that time, there was a purpose of acquainting myself with those fields. When I got all this big money soon, I was going to invest it in cattle. I needed to know these wheat fields existed so I could seek them out at some point to lease and run my cattle. Then, all of a sudden this power within me would direct me to turn around and go back the other direction. It was strange how I felt, like I was being directed on where to go, but I felt like it was necessary to do as I was instructed.

While we were at the stock show, several other freaky incidents happened that me, my wife, nor our friends could explain. I was very short tempered. I would jump on my kids or wife and it didn't seem to matter to me who was watching.

My mind had started changing its focus. I realized that the company that I started out trying to build was a false front for a bigger purpose. This power within me told me that I was to partially change my focus from not only the business, but as I met people about the business, I was to get their name and write it down in a note book I carried. I carried that note book everywhere I went. I would meet strangers, look into their eyes, and if I felt impelled to I would ask their names and write them in my note book. I was to make a judgment call as to whether they were worthy to go to heaven.

Meanwhile, because of this huge amount of money I was about to receive, I wanted more land and cattle. I'd see a sale bill for a cattle sale in Missouri, so I would prepare to go to that cow sale. I'd tell my wife and parents that is was where I was going, when this power within me would change my direction to somewhere in the opposite direction. I don't think I ever got more than fifty miles from home on any of these outings. During these outings I would approach people that would need help. I was extremely generous with my money. I thought I was going to be rich pretty soon. I remember stopping at a convenient store. There were two young women and a baby in their car right in front of the door to the convenient store. They had their car door open and the baby was crying. As I walked by, I stopped and ask them what was wrong? The driver told me that her baby needed milk and she didn't have any money. I handed her a $10 bill and told her it was from God. Over the next several days, many things similar to that happened to me.

I had so much confusion in my mind by this time that I had turned against my brother Carl and a neighbor. My brother and I had always been very close, but for whatever reason I started hunting him down to do bodily harm. I didn't carry a gun, or wasn't a mean person in general, but I meant business with my brother, if I could only find him. I drove over to his house about fifteen miles from my home, on two separate occasions looking for him. Thankfully, my wife had alerted him to stay out of my way.

I was deceived by this power within to think that I was working directly for God. This note book became for a particular purpose. If I wrote their name in that note book, that meant they were going to heaven. All during this time, my mind was telling me that I had a mission to carry this note book and try to get as many people's name in it that I could.

This yearning inside of me to go on this mission became stronger and stronger. My mother and daddy got involved siding with my wife, telling me that I needed to get psychological help. I told them they just didn't understand. I told my dad, standing in his living room, that I had to take this mission wherever God wanted me to, even if it meant giving up farming. It was the season to be preparing my land for planting, so true to my dad's work ethics and knowledge, he started directing my hired hand on what to do, and between those two they kept my farming duties going, thankfully. I believe that my brother Lyndal helped prepare and plant my crops as well. I was so far out of reality that I honestly don't know who all was involved, but I am very thankful for each of them helping my dad save my farm.

Sometime about then, I had got enough people involved in my pyramid that I had in mind that I was about to receive a downfall of money. Every day, I expected it to just show up in my bank account. I went to Durant and bought a new truck. I told them I'd be back for two more new trucks in the next few days. At this time, my wife had detected that I was having serious problems, so she started making phone calls to our banker, the dealership, and also the law enforcement; warning them that I was not myself. She asked the dealership to not let me buy any more trucks. I took my brother-in-law and my nephew with me to drive those two additional trucks home. I was buying one for my dad and one for my brother-in-law. When I got to the dealership they told me that my banker had contacted them and told them I didn't have enough money in my account, so I better wait. Oddly enough, I accepted that and we came back home. My thinking was, I'd have to wait a few more days on my money to fall out of the sky. It just hadn't had enough time to be deposited yet.

Somehow God also inspired my wife as to who to call to start trying to get me some help, even though I refused to get help on my own. Her mother and dad were praying for me to be healed and come to my senses. Then, they decided that may not be how they were supposed to pray, so they changed their prayers to ask God to help the law enforcement to help shut me down before anyone got hurt. By this time, I was really getting out in outer space with my thinking and my actions.

She, by the grace of God, was led in the direction to seek somewhere that I could get Christian psychological help if I could ever be stopped. The right phone calls and leadership paid off for her. She stayed one step ahead of me, whatever I tried to do. Between her and God, they had blocked my path so it didn't destroy our finances, or get someone hurt.

I had gotten very religious, but in a strange way. My mission was to be sneaky. I was God's secret weapon to move among the people, to see who was worthy to go to heaven. I had been deceived by the power within me that I was allowed to do anything, because I was working for God. I began to talk vulgar around my wife and mother, which I would never dare to do around my mother before. I had too much respect for her. By this time, my condition deteriorated to the point I decided that Jesus Christ had come down to earth and entered my body so he could move around discreetly, and this note book eventually became the book of life. If their names went in it, they had a place reserved in heaven. The vulgar talking was to fool people so people couldn't figure out it was actually Jesus.

I felt like I was indispensable. I could say or pretty much do almost anything and it was alright, like I had a free pass, or get out of jail free card. I had become infatuated with two particular local girls, both were from seventeen to twenty years old. I was acquainted with both, and they became an obsession. In my mind, God was going to allow me to have a relation with them both, even marry them along with my wife as a gift or reward for doing this deed for him.

My last few days before my capture was focused on where to find each of the young girls and begin my relationship. I never intended to harm either of them. I had in my mind that both of them wanted me to find them and rescue them. I thought they were being held against their will. I thought they wanted me to rescue them from their families. My desire was to love them and take care of them, and my wife was to approve of it. Both of the parents of the two girls saw that I was pursuing them, and they became very defensive trying to protect their daughters, and keep them away from me. Rightfully so.

During the last several days, I was seldom at home. I was roaming, hunting these two girls, night and day. I didn't sleep hardly at all, going anywhere I could to find them. I remember going to a house where I thought one of them was. The door wasn't locked, so I let myself in. I went inside the house in the darkness, in the middle of the night. The home was lived in by a cowboy family, had three boys which were all bronc riders and bull riders, so when I got inside and let my eyes focus, or there may have been a dim light, what I saw were several cowboys on pallets sleeping in the living room. I didn't see her, so I left without waking anyone up. On the outside of the home, there was different pieces of equipment and a propane tank. Around and among those items, I could see black beings, like demonic images. These images were not only at that house, I was seeing them in other places as well. I had even seen them in my own house. They appeared to come in through my windows.

During my outings in those last few days, the families of these girls were calling the law on me, so the law officers would stop me and search my truck for weapons and question me. Oddly enough, up until the last day or two I could fool most people. My middle brother Lyndal never could tell that I had anything wrong with me, but he wasn't directly involved with me daily.

I remember going to a rodeo about fifty miles from home, looking for the other girl who's family members were participants in the rodeo. I found her and visited with her for a few minutes. I walked around the crowd and visited with individuals asking about their horses, and how much they were worth and such. At some point I did something, my mind was in such a state by then, that I don't remember much more. The only thing I remember, I was standing in front of the crowd and yelling to them. I have no recollection of what I said, or what I did. I don't know if I cursed at them or pulled my clothes off or what. I will never recall what actually happened.

I believe it was that same night I went to that same girl's parents house in the middle of the night looking for her again. By this point all the laws were alerted to watch for me and what was going on. My wife had done a good job getting everyone up to date, to a degree. She just couldn't keep up with my movements.

At the door of the home, I believe I was met by her mother, and not to my knowledge, either her brother or her father had a shotgun pointed at me on the other side of the door. I found that out later. They called the law and within a short time the deputies showed up.

I remember standing on the edge of a gravel road in front of the house when they approached me. They took me down to the ground, planting my head onto the gravel road as they cuffed me. I remember that very well. I had just bought a new cowboy hat, which when my head hit the ground it crushed the crown on it. The most memorable part that I remember is at the same time they cuffed me some kind of force and loud noise came from within me, and out my mouth. It sounded terrifying even to the deputies, it sounded like a loud bull or beast bellowing. A sound I've never heard before, or since. It had such force when it came out of me that it blew the gravel and dust across the road with force, for several feet.

Whatever it was, it was freakish, loud, and powerful. That is what I vividly remember about it, plus one of the deputies that cuffed me was a family friend and he told my wife later that same story. That is the way he described it to her as well. It was nothing like he'd ever heard before.

I knew most all the people that were involved with my activities in those last few adventures pertaining to both girls, with exception to the rodeo crowd. As far as I knew, the only ones there that I knew was the family of the girl that I was looking for, whose father was a local veterinarian that I had previously used at times. Later, when I had recovered for a while, I asked him what all I did at the rodeo that day, and his reply was, "You're better off not ever knowing." So whatever it was, if anyone who reads this book, who were present that day, please forgive me. I don't have much memory of that day, but I was definitely not myself, and I am sorry for anything I did disgraceful, or for any other actions.

The deputies placed me in a jail cell in Madill, Oklahoma, and during my arraignment I remember telling the judge a few things that allowed him to see I had problems. I think I told him I was going to marry those two young girls and my wife was okay with the idea. Another thing I told him, was that if I wanted to, "I could point my finger at him and blow him out of his seat. God had given me the power to do that." My wife also said that I asked the judge to go back to his chambers and pray about his directions for my life.

I was then sent to Sulphur, Oklahoma. They had special psychiatric rooms that were designed for people like me, and Madill didn't have such. When I was at Sulphur, I got it in my head that they were trying to poison me by shooting gas through the air conditioning vents in my room. I became violent, and knocked a hole in the wall of my room with my fist. I was determined to leave, so when they came in to try to calm me down I made a break for the door and started down the hall. They told my wife that it took six men to get me back into the room. They said I was super strong. I weighed about 240 pounds at that time and was pretty solid, but I wasn't that strong without something inside me helping give me extra strength.

They strapped me down to the floor with buckles, both hands and feet. I couldn't move, I knew they meant business. I have allergies really bad, and my nose itches all the time. I can't go five minutes without scratching it. I was in a real pickle, I couldn't get a hand free to scratch, so I began to beg them to free just one hand. I promised I wouldn't try to escape again. They were gracious enough to finally free one hand so I could scratch.

I'm not sure how long I stayed strapped to the floor but they finally let me up after I promised to behave myself.

During that time in Sulphur I remember the thoughts of something within me controlling my actions, so I began to pray to God with more sincerity than ever before, for God to remove whatever it was that had control of me. I remember standing in the middle of that room, and while I was praying, starting at the top of my head, it felt like a clarity and relief started from my head and was draining down slowly toward my feet. I could feel a difference come over me. It almost felt like I was bleeding out, from top to bottom. I honestly believe with my prayer, God removed what ever was controlling my life at that point.

Debbie had the arrangements made already for me to be accepted at a Christian based mental hospital in Midwest City. From Sulphur, I was transported to that facility. The judge ordered me to stay there for twenty one days for evaluation. I remember the deputy that transported me from Sulphur to Midwest City drove about ninety miles per hour. I kept asking him if he was trying to kill us, so I was coming back to my senses by then.

My dad, hired hand, neighbors, and some of my brothers helped to plant my peanuts and kept the farm up to speed. I was so confused for months, I really didn't know who all helped. I am very thankful to have loved ones and friends that will help out in a crisis.

They put me on multiple medications, but ironically after the prayer I had with God in Sulphur to remove whatever was controlling me from my body, I was a different person. During my twenty one day stay in the mental hospital, I had an orderly tell me on numerous occasions, "I don't understand why you're even up here, you don't act like there is anything wrong with you at all." I remember one psychiatrist lady, I think her name was Karen. She held several group sessions with all the people under her care. She would ask questions to the group and I would answer all of them. She got mad at me for doing that and scolded me. I told her if she didn't want me to answer questions, she shouldn't ask questions. It made me mad, so I walked out of her class. She told my wife that I wasn't cooperating, that I wasn't giving anyone else opportunities. Most of the other patients were very quiet and reserved. They would hardly talk at all. I was the exception. I was alert and mentally aware of whatever she would ask and I think it intimidated her.

I can tell that as a humorous event now. The truth is, I was so mixed up and confused from living in a fantasy life for the past three months, I didn't know whether to stand up or sit down. I had seen so much and believed a totally different false truth for several weeks that the fantasy world had become my new normal. I was alert and not being driven by another power, but I was completely lost of what was real.

I was due to be released from the hospital on May 21. My sister had her wedding planned in Laramie, Wyoming on May 23, so the whole family was traveling to Wyoming. My wife had made arrangements to ride with some of the other family members, so my oldest brother Carl picked me up at the mental hospital. The one I had been threatening before, and I rode with him to Wyoming. I imagine he was a nervous wreck all the way to Wyoming, not knowing what to expect. I know that I would have been.

It was a tense time for all the family, because mental health is something that none of our family had dealt with before. For several weeks, then months, then a few years after that, my wife kept thinking I would have a relapse. I'm sure my parents, my wife's parents, and especially my brother Carl probably had a certain fear of that for a long time as well. The doctors told us that I would probably have reoccurring episodes. Every case they had treated before had.

To just tell this story sounds bad enough, but if you were my wife, my brother, or parents, they were scared to death during this ninety day period, not knowing who I would hurt or if someone would kill me, or how this tragic thing would play out.

It was almost more than my wife's nerves could stand. I think it almost completely wrecked her nerves. She had to start taking nerve medication during that period of time. My dad had to start taking nerve medicine as well to keep from having a nervous breakdown. This trauma is also why he got closer to God and got his life right with God, which included getting baptized. I mentioned earlier in this book that he had been saved when he was young, but never baptized.

When we got back home from Wyoming, I had to attempt to get back into society, and resume my farming duties. They had put me on a medication, where all I wanted to do was sleep. My hired hand would come into my bedroom and ask me questions. I was so lost about my own operation, I didn't know what to tell him. He had worked for me for three years by then and I was thankful he knew something about my farm, because it took me several months to actually resume my duties with some clarity. After a few weeks I finally told my wife they had to take me off that particular medication because I couldn't even function. She talked to the doctor and finally got me off that medicine. I think it was called Haldol. That may not be the correct spelling.

I was devastated when I finally got to thinking straight. I had been a very prideful person, nothing like that could happen to me.

It was the most humiliating, embarrassing thing that could have happened to me. I could hardly face the community. I just couldn't understand why this happened to Weldon Barnes, then I found out that my dad had gotten baptized while I was in the mental hospital.

My dad says that he's why I had to go through that, it was because of him. He had to have something to jar his world, to get his attention so he could see the need to be baptized. If that is true, then it was worth it. I wished my dad was still alive, and could read this book, because years later it became more clearly to me, that there were several reasons for me going through this. I really didn't feel like, at that time "I," was the reason that I had this experience, even though I had acquaintances tell me that it changed me as well. Some said that I had gotten pretty prideful, some said that they saw me as thinking I was better than others.

I'm not sure for what all reasons that I had to go through that. Sometimes I wonder about the other people whom I came in contact with throughout my ventures. If some of it could have benefited, in some way, someone that I never really knew. Was it partially for their sake? But I came to understand several years later, that a lot of it was for my benefit.

God has your number and if he thinks you're getting too big for your britches, for any reason, he knows the best way, the most effective way, to get your undivided attention. If I had given my testimony one year after this incident, it would have been completely different than it was seven years later, which was when I finally got the nerve to give my testimony to my church. I got up in front of our church, stood behind the pulpit, and all I could do for five minutes was cry. If my wife hadn't come up and held my hand, I don't know if I could have ever spoke to my church at all. It was still tearing my heart out from humiliation and embarrassment. I gave them an accounting of some of the things that I went through for the remainder of the entire service. I thanked everyone that had a part in keeping my farm work going, their prayers, and ones that helped my wife and family through this period.

If you can imagine, it literally took me seven years to sort out what was really real, and what I thought was real. I thought during those ninety days that I was the only one on the planet that knew God was using me for a very important job, and everyone else was in the dark, and it was as real to me as me sitting here writing this book. I was literally living a completely different life for ninety days. One example was, you remember that house that I walked into where all the cowboys were sleeping? I went back to that house shortly after I got home and even the shape of the house didn't even resemble the style of house I saw that night. I was totally seeing things differently than they really were on a lot of things. I was told that I went in certain places in adjacent towns, which I have no recollection of. My dad said that I sought out and researched his property deeds, which I also don't recall at all. I really have no clue what all went on with me and around me during that period of time. I remember parts of it, but I was so confused and messed up in my head that it took years to completely straighten things out in my mind.

There were several other encounters, small events throughout this period that I'm sure were significant to people, for better or worse. To anyone reading this book that had encounters with me during that time whom I offended, please forgive me. To me, I was all about trying to help people. In my mind I was invincible, and I felt better than I ever had before. I had the highest high you could have without alcohol or drugs. You really can't imagine what I had to go through to get my thinking cleared completely up afterwards.

I went back to farming my land pretty much immediately after I got out of the hospital, and most people had no clue how confused I still was, not even my wife. I could function somewhat normal, but I kept thinking the life I had been living was real, and it had to have meaning for my life. I couldn't just forget about what had transpired.

The doctors diagnosed me with bipolar disorder while I was under evaluation, so they had put me on Lithium for treatment. I went to a psychiatrist for several months after I got out of the hospital, as prescribed by the doctor. I'm not sure it helped me clear my head, but they do have a purpose. It may have helped more than I know.

I searched for answers, I prayed to God, and for years didn't seem to get any answers. I actually finally begin to realize that I had gotten my prayers answered from years earlier when I would pray for a strong testimony for my life, when I would hear someone else's tremendous testimony. God has delivered me from a traumatic event without me hurting anyone or anyone bringing harm to me. There were times and events from people holding guns on me, to me actually trying to harm my brother, and other things. I truly had a strong testimony where God saved me, and brought me through some very trying experiences. The only problem was, how could I use this testimony? If I try to tell people about me having mental issues, it would scare them to death. They would shun me and try to avoid me. Instead of being a good testimony, it would wreck my character.

In all honesty, in my mind, my character was already wrecked because of the episode I had experienced. I live in a small community, and almost everyone knows everyone. From that point on I didn't want to face people, didn't want involved in much of anything. I withdrew into trying to avoid social interaction. I lost my confidence. I was less of a man in every way. I can honestly say that I don't think that I have ever regained the confidence that I once had, even years later. In years past, I had been actively involved in our church visitation program. I have been blessed to help lead others to come to know Jesus Christ as their personal savior, but from this point on I could never witness face to face with people, partially because of my own conscientiousness. I knew in the back of my mind, I went crazy one time, so who would believe a crazy person? I had been a leader in our church as well in the community, but for whatever reason, I didn't think anyone wanted to listen to a person that had gone off the deep end.

I know God has performed a miracle in me to allow me to completely recover, but even now twenty seven years later, I still feel inadequate to witness to people. You would think it would give me the perfect platform to praise God, and I do praise him and thank him every day privately. When you talk to people, and tell them about you being mentally unstable once in your life, in my mind I feel like most people would still see me as mentally ill, or at least that is what goes through my mind. God gave me the prayer I ask for, a miraculous testimony, how God delivered me, protected me, protected others, and then did what I believe to be the super natural thing to allow me to come from totally nonfunctional in society, back to being normal again. None of my family members thought that I would ever get back into society as I have. I was truly messed up, and it was a miracle from God to heal me completely. God knows that I am very thankful for all the above, but it is still hard for me to use this story on a one-on-one witness platform.

Mental illness is something that no one knows how to act around, or respond to. People in that condition are very unpredictable and it scares most people to the point they'll do everything in their power to avoid being around someone like me.

About eight years after this event had taken place, I woke up in the middle of the night from a sound sleep, literally sobbing big tears. I could feel the Holy Spirit of God speaking to me, telling me that I needed to write a book about my experience, that someone else might benefit from it. By writing a book about my experience I wouldn't scare people by trying to tell them face to face. In my mind, it started to make some clarity finally, that this was part of God's plan. Maybe he was answering my prayers, giving me answers after all. At the same time I felt God's Holy Spirit talking to me about writing a book, I also got the impression that this was not the proper time. I was to wait about writing it. I couldn't understand that at the time.

I believe now, twenty seven years after the event in my life, God knew that if I wrote this book and the people around me found out what I thought happened, and that I had such strange far-fetched ideas, it would affect my living, and maybe destroy my livelihood, or someone would try to put me back in a mental institution. I also think my impressions to hold off were for another reason as well. During the past twenty years, all the things that have happened in my life has educated me to write a totally different book than what I would have written twenty years ago.

To be perfectly honest, I didn't get any indication that it was time to write this book until I was sixty five years old. At that time, God gave me the impression that it is now time to start preparing to write the book.

I am retired now from the public life, but continue to raise cattle on my farm, and God has blessed my wife and I with financial stability. I believe sharing my story at this stage of life will not have the negative implications on us like it would have had twenty years ago. I will describe some of those blessings I just mentioned in the coming chapters. I believe now that's part of the reason God had me to wait so long was for my growth and clarity of what I really feel like happened to me.

The following paragraphs are why God wanted me to wait til now. Some of you will think I'm still crazy, some will think I still need to be on medication, or may think I need to be locked up in a mental ward. I am sure some will probably think worse things than that, but this is my sincere belief of what happened to me.

This is where I may get in trouble with the readers of this book. My dad always claimed that I got brain washed by that pyramid company. I personally feel certain that I was introduced to a Demon, and he took control of my mind and body for that ninety day journey. It took me several years to come to that conclusion. First of all, I wasn't even sure I believed in demons in this day and age. I know there are several instances and documentation in the Bible about demons and God casting them out of people. I have read that many times, but the reality just didn't hit home in my brain. After years of studying and praying, I've come to realize that almost everything in the Bible that went on thousands of years ago in what we call the Bible days, still applies to today's world. Why couldn't demons be around us? I started dwelling on that aspect of this being a possibility. It wasn't something I realized at the time or even shortly afterward, I had to assure myself that I thought that could even be possible.

There are several things that brought me to that conclusion, but before I tell how I came to that conclusion I want the readers to know that if you have mental issues, please get and stay under a doctor's supervision for treatment. My circumstances were unique only to my case. Most mental health patients need to stay on medication at all times. Remember this, for the first nine years after my episode I was under my doctor's supervision continuously.

The first thing was that very strange relaxed feeling that came over me when that lady said her ritual. Next were all the encounters that I had with people as though I knew all about them. With some of them, it felt as though I was reading their mind. My wife and friends witnessed some of those encounters. The force within me that seemed to control where I went and what I did. The deceitfulness of the Demon was leading me to believe how I could talk vulgar, as well as marry those two young girls, and do anything I wanted without blame. It convinced me I was on a mission for God and finally convincing me that Jesus Christ was living within my body. The loud freakish bellowing, along with such tremendous force, that came out of my inner being as the deputies cuffed me, the fact that it took six men to overpower me to get me under control at the Sulphur hospital, and when I pleaded with God to remove whatever had control of my life. I felt as though that I was bleeding to death as something left my body. The fact that I felt completely different from that point on, and when that orderly kept telling me at the Midwest City hospital that I didn't act like, or appear to have any mental issues at all only a few days after I didn't even know where I was, and had talked so foolishly to the judge.

The final testament that has me convinced that it was a Demon is every person that I've known that has been diagnosed with bipolar depression, and I've known several since my episode, plus every care taker or doctor that I've ask the question to has told me that in every case of bipolar that they've treated, or have known about, has had reoccurring episodes. They normally keep having additional episodes. I have never had but the one, that lasted these ninety days.

Originally, I was put on Lithium for treatment which is a normal medication for bipolar. I was under my doctor's supervision and the dosage had to be taken three times a day, but I couldn't remember to take medication throughout the day, so after a short period of time of taking it correctly, I had not been very faithful to take my medication on time. That went on for several more years before I finally discussed this with my doctor. His reply was that "if I hadn't been taking a full dose of Lithium that I could probably be taken off it altogether." He said if I wasn't taking a full dose, that it wasn't doing me any good at all anyway. He said "that" particular medication has to be taken at the full dose, at a therapeutic level, or it didn't work at all. After approximately nine years, he took me completely off this medication, but I hadn't taken what they call a therapeutic level of dosage after only about the first few years. This testament is that I have not taken medication for bipolar depression for over twenty years, without any other episodes is a strong testimony that I don't have a bipolar disorder.

If you can imagine what my wife had went through as far as a traumatic experience throughout that ninety days, so when I came in nine years later and told her that my doctor was willing to take me off my medication, she went ballistic and said that wasn't going to happen, that she wasn't going through that kind of ordeal again. I finally convinced her to consider it, and ask her if she would go with me to my doctor's office and talk to him herself and allow her to ask him question. That was the only way she would finally consider me quitting my medication. She was very skeptical for several years afterward.

I cannot tell you for certain that I had a demon living within me for a short period of time. I even doubted my salvation because of my experience. I sought guidance from my father-in-law, the Baptist preacher, to discuss whether a demon could take control of a Christian's life. I was questioning many things. He told me that a demon could control the mind and actions of a Christian for a period of time, but he could not control my heart or control my soul. He said that my consideration of a demon taking over my mind and controlling what I thought, and what actions I took, was a very real possibility.

This is my father in law and my mother in law, J.D. and
Cleo Leavelle. I have as much respect for him as a very
humble and honorable man as any man I've known.

You don't know my father-in-law, and you may not agree with
his opinion on this matter, but I felt like he was one of the most dedicated Christians I have ever known. I had as much respect for him as
I did my own father. I knew him for over forty years before his death.
I never questioned anything he did, or said, to be anything but honorable, and admirable, and I never heard anyone speak of him other
than him being a fine Christian man. He sought out what was right,
sought God's leadership, and preached his heart.

In my opinion, demons are among us in today's society just like
they were in Bible times. They're controlling many people's minds
and actions in our society today. You can read newspapers and watch
the news. Some of the horrific and brutal acts that are being performed by some, couldn't be performed without demons controlling
their minds.

The Demon's residency in my mind was short lived, but it
caused so much confusion, doubts, and depression, I considered the
option of taking my life when I first started coming back to reality
rather than facing the community, my family, my friends, and my
church. Many things went through my mind for several months. I
am a living testimony that God's strength and Grace can heal you
from anything if you'll seek his guidance. I spent a lot of time in

prayer asking for his help, and gradually started feeling like my old self after several years.

My wife was my rock and my source of strength. She was loving, compassionate, and supportive. I told her several times, that if she had been the one having the mental issues, I wouldn't have been smart enough to realize what was happening to her, but her faith in God and her prayers led her to know that I had something unusually wrong with me and I needed help.

Another testament to God is how he was leading her to who to contact, and who to call to get the law enforcement to understand not to hurt me, that I had serious mental issues, as well as her having me a room and bed reserved at that Christian mental hospital in Midwest City. She literally had it reserved before the lawmen stopped me. I know only God could have given her those directions.

My father always said the pyramid company brain washed me, whatever that means. Some people says that my symptoms were relative to having a bipolar disorder, which with bipolar all cases I've ever heard about had reoccurring episodes, and you've also heard my thoughts of what I feel like happened to me.

Now, you have the privilege of determining your own conclusions of what happened to me.

CHAPTER 5

A New Era Of Life
Including Grandchildren

After I returned home from the hospital and started getting back into my regular lifestyle, looking at me, things looked pretty real to most people around me. I got back into my routine of operating my farm as usual, but I was still so confused about the things I'd seen, and the feelings I'd had during those ninety days. Life pretty much returned back to running my farm for the next four years and all the while I was still facing depression, not only because of all the trauma that had just happened, but because of feeling that we were still going to be forced out of farming. I kept searching for another source of income and ways to stay self-employed. My wife stayed on guard all the time. If I sneezed the wrong way she would question me, expecting me to have a relapse, or another episode.

In 1996, the first implementation of the NAFTA Trade Agreement went into effect with the new farm bill. It lowered the prices of the peanuts and corn to the point I really didn't realize much profit from that point on. Whatever I would borrow to make a crop on, I would pray that I would make enough money when I harvested my crop to pay all my notes. I was desperate to find other ways to make a living, and hopefully stay on the farm.

Since our kids had been showing livestock for several years, we had been up around the Oklahoma City Junior Livestock show and was able to witness companies where they would embroidery on caps, coats, and different articles. We decided we could do that in one of our bedrooms, so we bought a single head embroidery machine and went into business. My wife and son decided that Roadrunner Embroidery would be a suitable name for our business, so we were off to the races, as they say.

What we hadn't seen or heard of, was where these embroidery companies we saw at the stock shows were out in the everyday public trying to sell their products. From day one, my intentions, after acquiring some experience, was to go on the road with my line of jackets, caps, and designs, to FFA chapters around the state and offer our services to anyone interested. That was what I found catching about our name, Roadrunner, because I would be running the road, but of course, true to my wife being different, that wasn't her thoughts when she came up with the name at all. She said it just sounded like a cool name.

One thing I will caution anyone with a similar plan, make sure you know how to spell the right spelling of the same word. One of the first sizable jobs we were able to obtain was from a friend that owned a nursing home in Sulphur, Oklahoma, about thirty miles from our home. He asked us to sew one hundred caps that had his logo on it along with the name of the town, SULPHUR, on it. Well, being that I'm a farmer and I had put the chemical, Sulfur dust, on many different agriculture applications over the years. We sewed him one hundred caps with a single head machine, one at a time, and I set it up with the name of the town SULFUR.

We sent him the caps, and hilariously enough, he didn't notice the misspelling of the town until he wore one to the golf course and his friend brought it to his attention. That was a mixture of emotions. It was first of all embarrassing, but it was very expensive for us, new to the business with everything needing to work right, plus comical at the same time. Needless to say, we ordered more caps and stitched them properly, and delivered them to our friend as soon as possible.

Those misspelled caps ended up going to a good cause after all. My father-in-law, the pastor, was going on a mission trip to Africa shortly thereafter, and my wife and I sent those caps along with him to share with some of the people he would meet. They would be proud of them and had no idea that they had the wrong kind of Sulfur on them. My father-in-law said they were a big hit. The people were very pleased with them, so God does have a sense of humor.

As a perfectionist, as my wife calls me, I was not happy with the animals or some of the other patterns that you could order to be sown, and to me they didn't look like real animals. I wanted to be able to design my own animals, and any other design I wanted to, so when we bought our embroidery machine we also bought a software package, and a scanner to attach to my computer. I could actually scan any photograph onto my computer then digitize stitches to set it up to be sown on any garment.

Let me tell you a little about that particular application. When we went down into Texas and bought our first machine, we also got, along with the machine, eight days of training on how to digitize designs. I was such a country hick that I didn't even know how to turn on a computer, but I told them what I wanted the capability to do, and they sold me the right system. I came home and spent hours trying to learn how to make everything work. You talking about a country hick going to town. Everything about that, when we started was very foreign to me. But I was determined, and pretty soon I could put out some simple products. As I got more experience I soon started designing and sewing my own show animals, like hogs, calves and sheep on caps and jackets.

We grew our business fast enough that we outgrew the bedroom pretty quickly. I bought an insulated portable building and we set it in our back yard, hooked up electricity, built work benches, and everything we needed, and before long we were sewing enough that we had to expand again. My cousin was a carpenter so I hired him to add an additional building onto the storage building so we would have room enough for a larger machine, more working area and more storage. Then, we bought a four head embroidery machine that would sew four items at a time.

At that time, we knew we had to have some help, so we hired a local lady to help Debbie sew. I knew it was time to implement my original plan of taking it on the road. At that time I knew that in order to keep that larger machine busy, I needed to spread my wings. I had spent the past year or two learning the business, and more about setting up designs, and digitizing patterns, and it was time to broaden our horizon.

We begin taking an assortment of caps, jackets, and catalogs, to individual FFA chapters in the state.

At that time, as far as I knew we were the only embroidery company making personal visits to schools.

During the next few years we had several little league teams and other sporting teams, such as soccer teams, and such, asking us to make their uniforms. We couldn't feasibly compete with that business with only an embroidery machine. We started looking at screen printing options, and as God would deliver, Debbie had worked part time with a lady and she and her husband had a screen printing business setup, complete with everything we needed, so we bought that. They were nice enough to teach us how to operate it. We added that to our services we offered.

I would design new patterns if needed for the sewing, and by then I had hired another young man to help me on the farm and he was very good with a computer, so he would do most of the art work for the screen printing. After, my wife and her helpers would do the sewing or screen printing, along with our help at times.

Remember, I'm trying to grow this business, designing all the patterns and setting all the designs to be sown. Debbie didn't learn the software program, so I was responsible for all of that and at the same time still had the thirty eight brood sows, grinding feed for them, trying to condition show pigs, and take pigs to sales to market them all over the state. I also still had 150 registered mother cows, along with farming 350 acres of irrigated crop land. I had literally built up a business that I really don't know looking back, how I was able to do it all. I had some good farm help with my hired hands, which I couldn't have done it without them. Debbie, over our embroidery span had different women at different times helping her, but every aspect of our operation had to have me participating to a huge extent on all of it.

My oldest son had graduated in 1993 so he had left home, and was working on his own. My youngest son was helping part of the time when he wasn't in school. We had a full time job, to say the least. We really didn't have any down time or off season. Something was needing attention at all times. My youngest son graduated in 1998 and began his own life outside our home. We had built up our new business enough that we decided to pursue it full time, so I leased out my peanut quota pounds to a neighbor farmer. We spent that year working the embroidery and screen printing business, running cattle, and raising and selling show pigs. We made a living but didn't make enough extra money to pay our notes on our farm loans, so I refinanced my loans for the first time in my life.

The following year I went back to farming peanuts and corn along with all the other things. Without either of my sons involved in the show pig business I was losing interest about that time, considering selling out. One of my best friends had kids still at home and he was interested in raising pigs so we formed a partnership. He and his kids would do most of the work, but it still wasn't as interesting to me since I didn't have a kid of my own involved. My main responsibilities was to market the animals. I didn't pour my best efforts into marketing the pigs, plus the industry was changing rapidly at that time, so the end results, we didn't make much money. I had changed my breeding program up and started raising a different breed of hogs than what we had been previously successful with, even though my hog friend, the county agent discouraging that move, so it didn't work very well. My best friend and his kids tried it for two years and with no profit they had all of it that they wanted. I have always felt bad about that partnership. I know now that my heart wasn't in it, and I didn't put forth as much effort and energy as I should have. I would like to apologize to that friend of mine for my actions. I have tried to make up for it to some small degree since then.

On January 10, 2000, one of the most important things came about. My first grandbaby was born, and she was a precious gift from God. The first girl in my immediate family. She was the most precious thing to me that a Papaw could receive. A lot more happened that day, when my little angel was born than any of my family knows about. Something I have never shared with anyone before now. Not taking anything away from my sons or my wife, because I love them dearly, but after I recovered from my episode in 1992, for the next eight years I really didn't care if I lived or died. The embarrassment and humiliation was almost more than I could bare. I hum drummed through everyday life, while suffering from depression. I felt like my character as a church member, as a father, and husband was pretty shameful, because I felt like a failure, and less than a man. My life to me was pretty much useless I felt.

By the year 2000, we had sold the hogs off the place. I had lost some of my leases so my cow herd had been cut in half. Another testament about what dad had told me when I was fifteen years old, "You can't keep leased land for very long at a time." Some sold, others their family members took it over. One owner had a man offer him more for his pasture than I was willing to pay.

When Rylee, my granddaughter was born, my life became important again, I could see brightness in the day again. I wanted to live again. Rylee needed me as a Papaw, but worse than her needing me, I needed her. I had a new reason and purpose to get up and get busy every day. I want her to know how special she was for more than just a granddaughter, she resurrected my self-worth.

The hogs were gone and the cattle numbers had shrunk to about half the numbers. The crop prices were shrinking to the point of no profit, so our livelihood had started spiraling downhill. You wouldn't think things could get much worse, but it did. At the beginning of the crop year of 2000, a chemical company was advertising a new weed chemical to be used on peanuts. It was called Strongarm. I had attended meetings and heard the propaganda on it. It looked like it would take care of a new weed that had started showing up in our fields just in the past couple years, but being it was new I was somewhat cautious. I applied it to some of my peanut fields and left it off others. As the growing season progressed I could see a difference in the peanut vines that had this new chemical on them. I called out experts to help me determine whether it was the new chemical. Everyone agreed it was the cause. I started documenting everything throughout the summer. When we harvested the crops, the peanuts having this Strongarm on them yielded about 30 percent less in production.

I contacted the chemical company, and provided them with my proof from my other fields that didn't have the Strongarm on them. About that same time, everyone in the country had determined that their crops were damaged because of this chemical. The result was that a class action law suit was drafted. The lawyer heading that suit called me and said he had been told that I had documentation of real proof of comparisons that this Strongarm had damaged my crops. He said I was the only one out of one hundred farmers affected by this chemical that had documented the summer growing season. He begged me for my proofs, and said it would help win the case for all one hundred farmers.

Meanwhile, the chemical company contacted me. I had calculated the damage to amount to a $35,000 loss on my crops that year. They agreed to pay me that much damage if I would turn over my documentation and not join the law suit. I had a hard decision to make. I could get back my losses in full, or I could join the law suit and try to help the others. I felt more loyal to my fellow farmers than I did to a chemical company, but it wasn't an easy decision for me. I needed that money, so I studied, and I prayed what would God have me do. I was really struggling whether to save my own losses for sure, or take a chance on getting anything out of the law suit. The lawyers were filling me full of false hope telling me that they would win the law suit, and I would wind up with four times the amount of money in the end. That was bearing on my mind and I felt somewhat obligated to help my fellow farmers out because I knew they didn't have any evidence to prove the chemical was the cause. According to this lawyer, without my evidence they didn't stand a chance of winning. All the farmers well-being was riding on my back. It wasn't a comfortable position to be in.

A freakish and stupid thing happened about that time that ended up teaching me one of the most important lessons of my life. I had prayed for days for God's leadership and didn't seem to get any direction. I was eating at a oriental restaurant, and when I finished eating I opened up a fortune cookie. The fortune in the cookie read as if it was speaking directly about my decision on this matter. I don't remember what it said, but it lead me to believe my best option was to join the law suit and try to help my fellow farmers, so I called the lawyer and handed over my evidence.

Over the next several months there were several meetings, then finally a federal hearing. During the hearing, the Federal Judge's remarks included, in simple language, that a law had been passed about twenty five years earlier that protected chemical companies and other big cooperation from law suits from matters such as this. It was due to this being an experimental chemical so the chemical company didn't owe anyone anything. Most of the farmers lost 30 percent of their crops and didn't get anything for their losses. I finally got about half of my losses recovered. It was hard for me to accept that was what God had planned for the outcome, but after time and lots of praying, I concluded that God was teaching me a lesson. The lesson that I got out of that experience was, that to determine my decision of which way to turn from a fortune cookie was foolish, so because I did that I got just what I deserved.

The experience also taught me to not be a gold digger, not to wish for more than what is fair. If someone is trying to be fair with me and pay me back my exact losses, take it, and thank God for just getting that recovered, but I still have felt good about trying to help my fellow farmers. We all got cheated and deceived, and I came out better than most. Life is complicated, but I had just lost $17,000 because of making the wrong choice. At that point of my life it was a very bad time to lose money, but life is full of lessons. Some will knock you down, but I guarantee you I will always remembered that lesson. The truth is, if I had that same decision to make all over again it would still be very difficult for me not to try to help my fellow farmers recover part of their losses. I still feel like it was the right thing for me to do even though it was costly for me. I feel good about my decision and God has helped me to recover in other ways, but I still don't have good feelings toward that chemical company.

Things were looking pretty grim by this time. We kept farming peanuts and corn, and running the embroidery and screen printing business for the next two years, but we owed a lot of money. When we started the embroidery business we borrowed a lot of money to get it going, as well as refinancing our farming operation so needless to say, we were starting to sink. We were still treading water, but things weren't looking good.

For the past six years, my wife had worked her fingers to the bone hooping, sewing caps and garments, and standing almost all day. For the past three years she had begun to have problems with her muscles and joints. She went to an arthritis doctor. They diagnosed her to have Fibromyalgia. They put her on medication, but it still didn't give her much relief. She worked with stiffness and soreness all the time.

We had grown our business and increased our production trying to get it big enough to make our living and pay our notes, but we realized we couldn't do that in our back yard. We needed a store front in a town. I began looking everywhere for a building to lease in three different towns around us. I would get a lead on a piece of property and pursue it until something would block me, then I'd go another direction, to another, those would be blocked. I checked into buying a block of land to build on in a town where we felt like the location would be good to move our business. I tried buying buildings, still something would block our progress. I realized I hadn't included God in our pursuit, and nothing seemed to be working. I began to pray about what God would have us to do. What direction would he have us to take. There were still no results.

I had also felt that a lot of Debbie's health issues was from all the physical work she had done for the past six years because she kept telling me that her symptoms weren't really the same as what she felt like would be for Fibromyalgia. Debbie is the type of person that she would almost kill herself, with no sleep, to get products out on time, so she wasn't getting enough rest. She would work til all hours of the night and get up and go again the next morning. Ever since we had been married, Debbie had required more sleep than most people do. If she got run down because of lack of sleep and rest, she would just shut down. It would make her sick, then if she could catch up on rest she was good to go, but it would affect her physically, just because of not getting enough rest.

This was taking place in the late spring in 2002. I found out about that time that the new Farm Bill was going into effect one year early, and they would implement the NAFTA Trade Agreement into full force that year. This would completely take all my profitability out of my crops. By that, I knew this was my final harvest and final year to try to farm peanuts and corn. I wasn't seemingly getting anywhere trying to relocate our business, so that last year of farming was extra stressful to say the least.

I felt very defeated about my life because I was planning on farming until I died or retired. I thought having to change occupations at the age of fifty was a disgrace, and I really didn't have any focus on life. I thought quitting farming was the most devastating thing that could happen to me, but I knew I had to do something different, because for the last six years all I was doing was spinning my wheels. I wasn't getting ahead at all and was actually getting a little farther in debt each year.

As I would pray, I finally realized all the doors I was trying to open to relocate our business were getting slammed in my face, and the fact that Debbie's health had deteriorated because of the work involved with our business, I realized that God might have a different plan for our lives. Maybe we weren't supposed to move or even stay in that business at all.

My stress level was peaking again. We were going to be desperate by the fall of the coming year so I started praying to God for his leadership. What will I do to make my first note due in the fall of 2003? God started delivering my next step in life. With my prayers, God helped me figure out the only way that might work would be to buy a semi and go into trucking. I had run farm trucks, but didn't know how to even shift the gears on a semi. I went to a local truck mechanic shop just to discuss what kind of truck, what kind of transmission the mechanic would recommend. Even what kind of business I should look into. I didn't know anything about that line of work at all. I had been on my farm since I had graduated from high school thirty two years earlier.

You can see the power of God when he has a hand in your life. I went into the owner's office and started my line of questioning.

There was a man sitting in a chair off to the side in the owner's office. He asked me if I would be interested in a bobtail truck. Not a tractor-trailer rig, but a semi with a box bed that lifted and dumped. He had been working for an asphalt company hauling rock, sand, gravel, and asphalt. He told me that I could probably even work for that same company he had been working for. His plans were to start a construction business building metal buildings, so he had his truck for sale. I went to his house later that day, he showed me how to run his truck, shift the gears, and such. I bought the truck in September of 2002 while I was still farming and preparing to harvest my final crop. I parked it out in my pasture. I didn't have CDL driver's license, so I couldn't even drive it legally at that time.

I knew God had that man sitting in that office at that exact moment, so when I came in I would meet him, and in turn buy his truck with an opportunity to put it to work. He educated me to a business of hauling for asphalt companies which would give me stability without running all forty eight states. I could stay in Oklahoma so I could still come home at night and take care of my farm. He also gave me some driving lessons at the same time, which I needed extremely bad just to get me started. Debbie and I discussed all our options. I wasn't going to farm row crops next year. We decided that Debbie would be better off just getting a job in town, which would help pay the bills while I began my trucking business, and would also provide us some health insurance.

We put the Roadrunner Embroidery business up for sale and before the end of the year we had buyers. They took control of the business January 1, 2003. I finished my last peanut harvest in the fall of 2002. By the Government implementing this program one year early and ending the program we had been on for the past six years, that action alone, actually cost me a $35,000 loss. We were supposed to have higher prices for one more year. When they put it into law early we sold our last crop on the lower prices.

To let you know what our status was on January 1, 2003, we had shut down the hog operation, my cow herd had been cut to about seventy cows, I was no longer farming any row crops after that fall, and we had sold our embroidery business. We had borrowed a lot of money when we started the embroidery business. We sold it at a much reduced price and we had to refinance our farm loans in 1998.

So to sum it up, we had seventy cows left to make income, we owed over $200,000 from farm and embroidery loans, neither of us had a job, and we would have our first big note due in the fall of 2003. Like I've explained in this book before, I have a lot of pride and the last thing I would actually consider would be to file for bankruptcy, but due to my financial condition I really was worried about that becoming a possibility. I actually went and visited with an attorney about, "what if I can't make my payment, what would be the procedure," and such. I knew that would be my last resort. Talking about a stress level hitting the ceiling, I spent more time on my knees seeking God's leadership that fall and winter than I had ever before.

I give praise to God for the miracles he performed in my life over the next three years. I got my CDL driver license, went through some schooling, applied for carrier license for a trucking business, and in March of 2003 went to work with my truck at that same asphalt company that the previous owner worked for.

On March 13, 2003, another very important day of my life happened. My grandson was born, and he was another of God's precious gifts. One of the most heartwarming things about it, my son and daughter-in-law wanted to name him after my dad. My daddy's name was Calvin Dillard Barnes, and I had named my son Leland after me. We both share the same middle name, Leland Keith and Weldon Keith. They wanted to name my grandson after both Leland, myself, and my dad, so they named him Dillard Keith Barnes. I felt very honored.

Therefore, I had another reason I wanted to live. I began to pray, God please let me live to see my grandkids graduate school. They both need me, but I need them more. I wanted to share in everything they did. I had missed out on many things that my sons partook in during their teenage years because I was always working. I made a promise to myself that I was going to try my best to share in as many things my grandkids were doing as they would allow me to do. My goal was to be involved in everything from birthday parties to all their sports, track and field events, as well as teach them how to hunt and fish. I wanted to just spend quality time with them. My dream was for them to cherish the times we would spend together throughout the years, and remember the good times and have special memories of their Papaw, because I know I was enjoying every minute of their young lives already.

From the time I took that trucking job at the asphalt company, I begin to feel more confident, but I hadn't seen the full scope of what God was really setting the stage for.

The prior fall when I harvested my peanuts I planted a winter crop of wheat and rye on my peanut ground. I bought 107 young heifers and put them on that winter pasture. The next spring I put bulls on them and got them bred, meanwhile I was running my truck, coming in and taking care of my farm. I was taking off work for a few days at a time to cut and bale hay. I was working many hours a week. It paid off in the fall of 2003 when I sold those heifers through a replacement sale. They made very good profits. I was able to pay not only my note, but I paid extra on my notes.

That fall, fall of 2003, I had an order buyer buy me eighty-five young open cows. I put bulls on them and got them bred. Meanwhile, I had seen how much more money I could make if I owned an eighteen wheeler. I could haul almost double the load, and make more money with the same amount of fuel. In the spring of 2004, I bought a tractor-trailer rig. I visited another asphalt company in Shawnee, Oklahoma, to see about working for them. They hired me and I began making a lot more money. I bought another truck to haul grain and put a driver in it. It made a little extra money to help.

That next fall, fall of 2004, I sold those young cows through a replacement sale, and they doubled their money. I was able to pay a lot more extra on my notes. I was running my truck sixteen hours a day trying to make all I could with it. At the same time, my cattle were making good money. I wasn't spending a lot of money because I was sitting in that truck all the time.

My wife had gone to work and was helping pay bills. She first worked at a local bank in the beginning of 2003, and worked there for a few months when a local home health and hospice company called her and ask if she would be interested in a job. She accepted the job. That company was owned by a very fine Christian couple. She was working with good people and my wife loved her job. Her health begin to improve since she had quit the embroidery business. We decided that the stress of making deadlines, and the hours on her feet, all the hooping and straining on those frames, was more her diagnosis that having a disease like Fibromyalgia.

God was showing me his power because I believed in him, and sought his leadership. Within three years of trucking and buying and selling cattle, God helped me get almost all of that $200,000 debt paid off.

I can honestly say that three years went like a blur. I cannot tell you how all of that was possible. Sure, I worked my behind off, trying my best and working long hours to accomplish that, but I give God all the credit for showing me the way, giving me the management skills and such, and opening the doors for all of that to be possible.

There was one key ingredient that I feel like made this possible that I haven't discussed. When the government shut down our peanut program, they paid me for my peanut quota pounds. A sizable amount of money, but I owed several times more on my notes than I received from the government. I spent a lot of time seeking God's leadership about that money. Should I pay it all on my notes, or pay my tithe on it. It was an arguable matter. It really wasn't earned income because I had bought my peanut quota pounds over the years myself, so I didn't really feel that it was a certain obligation to tithe my 10 percent, but I felt I needed to do just that. I paid my 10 percent to our church. I trusted God that if I would pay the tithe on it, he would help me through this hard time.

I also figured if I paid all of those proceeds on my notes, I could have a cushion for a few years and maybe come up with a plan to pay off the rest later, but God helped me figure a better way. Instead of paying all that money on my notes, I made one payment. With the rest of the money I bought those heifers, bought the semi, and truck fuel. I have heard it said in church all my life that you can never out give God. I am living proof that if you'll trust in God and pay him what is his share, he will see you through anything.

In 2005 I had my debt paid down to a comfortable level, so I sold my extra truck and hired a driver to run my truck, then I went through schooling to get my real estate license and started selling real estate.

I was never meant to be a trucker. I like to be at home at night and spend time with my family. My grandkids had gotten big enough that I wanted to be at home to share in their lives.

My grandchildren, Rylee and Dillard.

My whole life had been surrounded with a very close family, my entire family was still very close, and family was very important to me.

My brothers, sister, myself, mom, and dad in 1994
as we celebrated their 50th wedding anniversary.

I began to look back at my life in the past thirteen years since my episode. We had many hardships, looked dangerously close to going broke, went through three or four different businesses, and were forced out of the farming business; which I loved and thought I would be involved in until my retirement, or death. Here we were, in a totally different environment, thirteen years later. Making our living off the farm.

I began to look at the tracks that I had laid out over the past thirteen years, thinking about the doors that were opened, and the other doors that were slammed in my face. The people and events that were instrumental to get me from that point of my life to this one. It was very evident that only God could have helped me follow those paths, opening the doors, and yet shutting others to turn my direction or force me to depend on him for guidance. To me, it was little miracles that God was performing all through that journey for little ole me. You can't see what is happening many times, but God is always there. You may not be heading in the direction that you thought you wanted to go, but if God is at the wheel, you will wind up in a good place when the tires stop turning.

When I finally got out of the truck, I began sleeping better than I had in years. We were pretty debt free, I didn't have to lay awake at night trying to figure out what me and two other hired hands needed to be doing worst, or first, the next day. When you're trucking, there is never enough sleeping time. For three years I would leave home about 4:00 a.m. to head to a rock crusher plant to start loading, and many times it would be 8:00 p.m. or later by the time I would get back home. I would clean up, go to bed, and at 4:00 a.m. be gone again. When I got out of the truck I almost felt like I was on vacation. God had given me a new peacefulness in life. I had two wonderful grandkids, my wife was loving her job she'd had for a couple years at that time, and my stress level was finally letting up to be able to enjoy life again.

Three years earlier I was thinking what a disaster it was to have to quit farming, but in reality it was the best thing that could have happened to me. I feel like now that God allowed me to be forced out of the only livelihood I'd known to show me how much power he had if I would only trust in him. If I'd stayed in farming, I doubt that I could have been able to overcome that indebtedness. I probably would have had to file for bankruptcy. My life since farming has had much more peace of mind, a lot less physical work involved, and he has provided means for me to make a living without working so hard. It's strange the way things look at times, and then looks after you have come through it. The same situation went from devastating to miraculous in three years.

This is the last portrait that my mother and father made
before his death in 2004. They were married for 60 years.

Because of the trauma and all the many, many different struggles that had taken place in the past thirteen years, I feel like I owe my two sons an apology for not being there for them a lot of the time while they were teenagers. That was the period of my life where I was trying to grow a business. The year my oldest son started high school, 1989, was the year that my stress level went through the roof because of the NAFTA Trade Agreement. It stayed that way all the way through Leland's graduation in 1993, and continued through

Nathan's graduation in 1998. Those years were when I had the worse work load trying to keep from going broke, plus trying to add other things into my operation to help overcome the losses of what the new farm bill had taken away. The worse possible timing for raising my sons. I am sorry that happened at that exact time of their lives.

I know my sons weren't aware of all the struggles my wife and I were having trying to stay on the farm. They wouldn't have understood or been able to grasp the seriousness of it anyway. My prayer is when they read this book maybe they can hopefully understand a little better what I was going through, and somewhat of a reason for me being the way I was. As adults now, they have faced struggles of their own.

I think the stress caused me to be very impatient with my sons. I expected perfection in whatever they did and wasn't satisfied with anything less. That was the way I was raised, and it fit me pretty well because I wanted to be a perfectionist, but it took me several years and growing and watching other people to realize that not everyone wants to be that way. I realized after it was too late, that it wasn't necessary to do everything near perfect.

I made many mistakes as a father, but I tried teaching them the way I was taught, as well as the way I thought would teach them the best way to make it through life, but I think I carried it too far by expecting too much from them.

My sons called me a workaholic, and that's what I was during the period of their life when they were wanting to have fun, probably to the point that they didn't even want to be around me, because I would put them to work if they hung around me very long. There was never enough time in the day to get all the things done during that period of my life.

The problem is, I can't ever get any of that time back, it's lost forever. So to my two sons, I'm very sorry that my life got so complicated during your growing years, and years that I should have been there. I should have been more patient with you also. I'm very sorry.

I don't know if what I taught them had anything to do with it, but they both can build things and get it done plenty good on their own now. I have seen some of their projects that they've built and put together and they did a good job with it. One example, was Leland, my oldest son, decided to build him a rack or rail structure out of square tubing and mount big lights all along it around the front and sides of his boat so he could lean against it while he bow fished while standing up. It had several difficult corners and 45-degree connection to be welded together. He did a very nice job building it. He also built folding blinds out of tubing frames and artificial shadow grass and built connections to mount on his boat for duck hunting. He can build whatever he needs to get the job done. I've watched things my youngest son Nathan has done as well, and he also has the ability to do whatever he needs to.

I know when they watch me with the grandkids sometimes, I'm sure they feel like I have deprived them, because I spend a lot of time with the grandkids, spend money on them, share in almost everything they do, go to almost every function or ball game they have, but I hope they can understand after reading this book. There are many reasons for my actions.

It's not that I love my grandkids more than I loved my sons when they were that age. It's because I'm older, not as stressed, and have more time. I see a real need and desire now to spend time with my grandkids, that I didn't see before, but at the same time I didn't have the time to spend at that stage of their lives. I hope they understand. I still love my sons, and am very thankful for them. I am also thankful that I have slowed down enough now to share in my sons lives whenever possible and if they choose, as well as my grandkids functions.

CHAPTER 6

Real Estate Business
A New Career

In 2005, I went to work for a nice real estate broker in an adjacent town. She taught me the ropes about the business and was nice enough to share the phones with me to help me start my business. The real estate business, for those who don't know, is either feast or famine. That was one of the first things I was taught. If you have a good year and make a little extra money you better store it away, because the next year may be a famine.

One of the things that I will always remember about that first year, I had several friends tell me that I would become a crook being involved selling real estate. I would ask them why they felt that way. Their reply, was that they hadn't known many honest real estate agents yet. They said there was too much temptation to get your fingers dirty. I told them that I had never been a greedy person. I was honest and if I had to become corrupt to sell real estate I would get out of the business. I told them that I would treat people like I would want to be treated and that I could sell property without getting my fingers dirty, that I would always be honest, and have integrity.

I didn't know people felt that way about real estate agents when I started selling, but it didn't take too long to start seeing and appreciating what they were saying.

Many of the other real estate companies that I would try to work with, or co-broke with, some of their agents would try to steal your customers away from you, and at times actually did steal them away. They would sneak around behind your back and make deals with customers that I had brought before them. It was a corrupt business.

I had been sheltered from the public all my life until I got into trucking, three years earlier. I had been on my little farm for the most part, been self-employed, and hadn't dealt too much with the public life. I soon was schooled, really fast, on how selfish and greedy many people are. They would do anything for a little more money. That didn't set well with me, but I finally had to come to terms, "that it is what it is." My friends that told me about not knowing honest realtors was pretty accurate. You deal with a little of that even in the farming business. It's in every avenue of life, but I had rarely seen that side of people until I had started driving a truck three years earlier. I learned in the trucking business, that there were certain people that were greedy and they would try to run ahead of you or steal your loads.

The worse thing I experienced, was if you got a little side line hauling for someone other than your normal company and asked a fellow trucker to bring his truck along to help you one day, before you knew it he would undercut your prices just enough to take over your gig, then he would get his buddies involved himself.

I was limited on what I could do. I couldn't have gotten a good job anywhere else. I was overweight and my body was worn out from hard work and carrying too much weight for years. At that time I was fifty three years old, so I couldn't be too choosy. I really didn't see that I had a choice but to stick it out. It was interesting work, along with the downside of the business. I didn't have to participate along with that side of the business. I kept my business honest, and with God's blessings I was able to make a living. The real estate, along with my wife working and selling my calf crop at home, we made it okay. We didn't owe a lot of money so it didn't take so much to survive.

About all we did for the next couple years was just get by. The reality of not having much to retire on begin to bear on my mind.

We had gotten out of debt, but we had been self-employed most our adult life, and hadn't been able to save any money so the worry started to set in again. Our retirement wasn't looking very promising at all. Neither of us would draw a very large Social Security check. That was the main reason I focused on becoming a real estate agent. Even into my older years I could sell property. As long as I could ride in a truck and write contracts, it was feasible to work as long as I was able. I felt like that would be a real likelihood at that time.

My broker helped me a lot to learn the business and I worked through her office with some nice people. One of the agents in her office was an elderly man. He was already retired from his occupation. He had always been in sales, throughout his life and he was a good salesman. I sort of attached myself to his shirt sleeve, became good friends, and learned from him a lot about the business. I always called that gentleman a blood hound. If he got on a trail for a piece of property, or got a buyer interested in something he was very persistent with trying to close the deal. He was honest, but he had been trained as a salesman, and there were little things he knew that could make the difference in persuading the parties to close.

I learned more from him than anyone and he was nice enough to help teach me, but I was always kinda shy, so I wasn't persistent enough. I could never be the salesman that he was. I never did like being pushy as a salesman, so I was not persistent enough. I didn't want people thinking I was coming on too strong or being pushy at all. I had always hated salesmen of any kind that were pushy. I was determined that I would not be that way.

Contrary to what my friends thought that I would do, by becoming corrupt and crooked in the business, I was the opposite. I was extra honest to my customers. Most salesmen would probably say that I was too honest.

I would have customers come from all over the country trying to buy cattle pastures. Many of them didn't know much about raising cattle and for sure didn't know the caring capacity of certain properties. If the seller would advertise that his property would carry one hundred cows on two hundred acres, I would be honest with my customer and tell them that wasn't right. I would explain the adequate carrying capacity.

In my business if I sold someone a property, I wanted to come back two years later and have them know that I had been honest with them. I didn't want them to be disappointed. I wanted them to know the truth about whatever I was selling. I have actually talked people out of buying something because I felt like it didn't fit them, or they were being deceived by someone else.

Sure, like any business, I would have customers that would mis-understand things, so I'm telling you, that I had unhappy customers at times, but I was always honest with them. I'm sure they didn't think I was at the time, but if you deal with enough people you will experience people you couldn't make happy, no matter what you did. In the thirteen years of selling property, I have seen a little bit of everything. When you are dealing with peoples' money you find out a lot about a person. Most of the conflicts I saw in people would almost always be stemmed from greediness in one way or the other.

Needless to say, I didn't get wealthy selling real estate, but I will cherish the friends I made during those times and the experiences I was able to partake in. My broker was always fair with me and she actually ran her business with integrity. If you worked for her you had to have integrity also. She wasn't tolerable of less.

I was still taking care of my farm and cattle at home. The real estate business gave me the opportunity to make pretty good money with limited time spent and limited expenses.

Over the next thirteen years I sold property part time, cut and baled hay, fed cattle, and spent a lot of time with my grandkids. Other than not having a lot of money, I was finally living the dream. My brother proclaimed I was semi-retired, and I guess I was to an extent. I was living a peaceful life for the first time in years, I could sleep good at night, and that was an accomplishment in itself.

True to my oath I took at Rylee's birth, my granddaughter, I was at every birthday party, soccer games, T-ball games, and everything else that she and Dillard had going, I was in the middle of it. The job that God had placed me in at that time, selling real estate, had given me the privilege and opportunity to set my own schedule. Rylee, more than Dillard was a sports nut. She wanted to participate in everything going on. She started playing soccer when she was little, and started playing t-ball as soon as she could. Then, on to playing basketball as a small girl at the church leagues.

Like her papaw before her, forty years earlier, she fell in love with playing basketball. She played a lot of Softball, ran track and field, and everything else going on during its respective season, but basketball was her passion.

She told me when she was about in the seventh grade, that her goal was to play college basketball, so I got her out in my back yard and taught her how to make a boy style jump shot. I told her that if she could get good with that shot and practice at it, that college teams would sure give her a look. I was old and fat and couldn't jump, because my knees were worn out, but I did the best I could to show her how to do it. I used to have a nice looking jump shot myself, back in the day. She developed a very nice boy style jump shot and got where she could hit the basket pretty good at the same time. As time went on she got better and better with her jump shot. She has had many people compliment her about how pretty her shot looks.

This is Rylee making one of her pretty jump
shots during one of her high school games.

Rylee has been encouraged by her entire family, by her mom and dad, Debbie, myself, and also helped some by friends around her home. Different ones have helped coach her and develop her into a very good basketball player over the years, but Rylee is to be credited for her own success. She is a very self-motivated person. When she sets her mind to do something, she will work as hard as possible to make it happen. She is a very good athlete because she worked hard to get to that point.

This is Dillard playing basketball in grade school.

I was also at most all of Dillard's birthday parties and school functions as well. As he grew, he followed in Rylee's footsteps. He played soccer, t-ball, and basketball, but he wasn't as enthused, or as much of an athlete as his sister was, but I was at most all of his functions nonetheless. Debbie would come to all that she could with her work schedule.

One of the things I am most grateful for is that God had placed me in a business to make a living with the flexibility to set my own schedule, to be off when I needed or wanted to attend my grandkids functions most of the times. There is no doubt that I could have made more money chasing real estate night and day, but the most important thing in my life was sharing in my grandkids lives as much as possible without neglecting my obligations.

As time went along during those years, Debbie and I had talked a lot about our retirement years. We were trying to figure out how we could survive after retirement. It wasn't going to be very glamorous for us. We had very limited income, but true to my wife's character she wasn't worried. Her motto was, "God will take care of us."

You would think after all that I had been through it would be that simple for me as well, but true to my nature I worried about something all the time.

In 2008, God delivered a very big surprise. Our next stepping stone, or more like an absolute gift. Oil companies started leasing up mineral interest in our area, as well as leasing some on our land. They drilled two wells, not far from our home, on a neighbor's property. I have a large irrigation pond on my place, so the oil company bought a lot of water from us to fracture those two wells. With the revenue we received from selling that water, God in turn laid it on my mind to take that money and buy some minerals in the surrounding area, in case they kept drilling multiple wells on different sections of land.

To help you understand the stress level about whether to actually use that money for that was very scary, because in the same year, 2008, we saw the stock market crash that sent the whole economy into a serious recession and, along with that the real estate sales had pretty much come to a complete halt. I wasn't making much money because people were too scared to buy anything, and for about the next three years, my sales were really low.

Along with that, we didn't have any money at that time, and finally God had blessed us with a significant amount of money. I had two choices, put it in the bank and save it, or buy these minerals, which was very risky. I had never researched for minerals in court house records, which is very difficult, and even if I could buy some, would they ever be drilled and be produced? The oil companies had drilled a couple wells in our area over my life time, over the past forty years, but just one here and there, nothing more. They had drilled only two new wells in our area at this time. All these thoughts were bearing on my mind when God brought a thought to my head. I remembered the saying, "you can feed a person fish for a day, or you can teach them how to fish and they will be able to provide for themselves forever."

So I stepped out on faith without much hesitation, and for the next few months I was in the court house searching for minerals to buy. They are very hard to search out in the court records, because they have been reserved and split so many times and in so many ways.

Very few people are willing to sell their minerals, even if you are able to determine who might own some. It was a dog fight, to search through those records, find someone that had a few, then try to locate the owner just to be rejected about selling them. I had to trace every tract of land back to the beginning of statehood, search all the deeds to see who had reserved them, and try to determine who actually owned the minerals.

My wife will witness that I would get so stressed digging through those records it would almost drive me insane. I spent hours of endless tracing. I actually came home after several days in the court house and told my wife, "I've got to stay away from there for a while." It was stressing me out so bad I began to get flash backs of messing up my mind, so I pulled out and got away from them for about thirty days. I got my mind cleared up and again went back to them.

The biggest problem is, it's like buying blue sky. There is nothing tangible to hold onto, nothing to borrow money against, nothing you can see. It was very stressful for me because of several of these reasons.

I finally was able to buy some additional acres of minerals. We couldn't afford too many, but those along with the ones we already owned that had been obtained when we bought our surface property, as well as inherited a few acres from my parents would be a supplement to our Social Security checks if and when they were drilled and started to produce. We were about ten years away from retirement, so there was time for all of these different things to fall in place.

Over the next year or so, they drilled wells on those properties where we had bought the minerals, and they also drilled an oil well on one of our properties.

I had dealt with the oil companies enough by then to know they weren't necessarily my friends. You had to stand firm while negotiating with them on anything they wanted to do, to keep them from skinning your hide off.

I knew from this experience by that time, that God guiding me into the real estate business was not only for being able to make a living, but God knew this oil business was coming to our area. By getting the schooling and education in the real estate business, I had been educated to reading legal descriptions, understanding contract laws, understanding townships, reading legal maps, and things like that which was very beneficial when dealing with the oil companies.

Since I was the only one of my siblings that had this kind of experience, they all looked to me to get the affairs of our family inherited minerals in order. Mom and dad had set up a trust in 1993, and that in itself became a nightmare to get all the oil companies records straight.

When you set up a trust, many times the records from that point on doesn't reflect clearly who is the rightful owners, or chain of title. It gets vague because things continue to change from that point forward, but doesn't necessarily get recorded and updated in the court records. Since the court records are the only place the oil companies can find these chains of events, which wasn't clear on my parents minerals, it became my responsibility to make sure they had everything in order. I had to send copies of several records to multiple oil companies, before getting all the loose ends clear to them.

Most of the upper management from these oil companies are very company minded. All they are interested in is getting what they want at the least possible price, and the property owners were not on the top of their priority list. As a matter of fact, I soon realized that for the most part, property owners were a necessary evil for them to have to deal with. You had to watch every move they made to keep them from running over you or taking advantage of you. After dealing with a few of these men, I became aware that it was just the nature of the beast in that business arena.

About 2010, I met a land man from an oil company. He was a blessing from God. He wasn't like the other oil company employees, he was very fair and he wanted to work with landowners, and when he wanted something from any landowner, he was willing to pay a fair price. He helped set new standards in this area and he earned my respect by being an honorable man.

There were other oil company employees that were somewhat fair. I'm not saying they're all too company minded, but this man was very fair. We understood each other and I learned to trust what he said. We had a good working relationship. Over the next couple of years and through working with him I was able to negotiate agreements with his company to sell them water, as well as negotiate deals to place two additional wells on our property. In the process of all these events, my wife and I began to build a nest egg.

Guess what? God was coming through again. We had no real means of a retirement a few years ago and with the inspiration of God encouraging me to buy more mineral acres, and with all the other things that had developed recently that God had provided, it was helping us become more financially secure.

You remember earlier in this book, when I said that God would place certain people and things in our paths to fulfill his purpose? God placed this man in my path in order to help my wife and I gain in financial security for our retirement.

I don't know if this man was a Godly man or not, but God used him to fulfill his purpose for our benefit. I know the man didn't realize what was taking place in that respect for our benefit until I told him later on. Nevertheless, this man was a good man, honest and fair with the people he dealt with. I pray for him still today, because I don't know his spiritual status, but he earned my respect and I know God used him for our benefit.

The sad truth, is that many people would look at these events as just luck. They would say, "boy those people are the luckiest people in the world for that to happen to them." Luck has had nothing to do with it. My wife has been right all along with her motto, "we don't need to worry, because God will take care of us."

Don't let that motto of my wife's deceive you though, she also believes that we all have to work very hard to do what is best for our families. She is not saying that you can just sit on your hands and

God will throw things your way. She has worked hard all of her life, as well. She just has the faith that if you work hard and do what you feel led to do throughout your life, God will provide for your needs. Her motto means, you don't have to worry about things that you can't help.

Another testament of this, I had said in 2008 we entered a very serious economical recession and my real estate sales came almost to a halt. I was struggling along, when in 2010 God provided me with another stepping stone. I have been overweight for several years, and I was introduced to a weight loss program that had a secondary benefit. I could join their business network and get other people involved to lose weight and become more healthy, meanwhile I could draw commissions off of the food they bought. That was another perfectly timed happening in my life designed by God. I was able to supplement my income with those commissions, along with a few real estate sales during those very trying years during that major recession. I was able to make enough to sustain a living.

It took the episode in 1992, the fear of being mentally incompetent indefinitely, the miracle of God returning me to my sanity and health, and other things in my life for me to start looking at life differently. The most important things to me since then are the little things. Spending time with my grandkids. A nice warm house to feel secure in, a good soft bed to sleep in, a beautiful wife to share my life with, and plenty to eat. It took growing in faith and watching God's hands at work in my life to start really appreciating the small things he provides for me every day. I took things for granted for years. I took my wife for granted, and didn't treat her with respect at times. I didn't see the importance of spending time with my two sons when they needed my time and efforts the most. Those are the two biggest regrets of my life.

I have made so many mistakes in my earlier years, and most of the time didn't even realize I was making them until sometime later in life. The truth is, I still make mistakes every day. I'm still not the kind of Christian I know I should be, but I am very thankful that I am looking at life with a different set of eyes in recent years. Now I can see the little blessings that God is performing in my life, every day.

CHAPTER 7

Consistency In Life

My local church has been my source of strength for years. I have been attending ever since I can remember. I gave my life to Christ when I was thirteen years old, so I have been a member there for fifty three years. In my lifetime, there have been many changes in our church, as far as faces. We have built up the church numbers for an average Sunday school attendance of 140 people, and down to about forty at different times throughout those years. Many of my loved ones and family members, along with many friends and neighbors that I admired have passed away as well. One thing that has stayed constant to me I feel, is where I hear about the Word of God, and fellowship with fellow Christians.

Back several years ago, I was very active in our visitation program and as I've said earlier, I have been instrumental in helping lead others to know Jesus as their savior. To me, there is no greater blessing than to know that you have helped in God's calling, by witnessing to others and watching them make the most important decision of their life.

I have served as the Sunday school director for a period of time. I have served on some of the different boards as well.

When I had my episode in 1992, for whatever the reason, that almost destroyed my willingness to approach people. I was so ashamed and embarrassed that I didn't want to face anyone, and sad to say, that part hasn't really gotten much better with time. It's the way I'm made I guess, but I am too self-conscience. That doesn't give me an excuse, because after almost twenty seven years, many people around my home town don't even know anything about what happened to me in 1992.

I feel that I should use that part of my testimony to witness to others, but I really don't know how. In my mind, if you give people a hint that you were once a mental patient, they still are very cautious of you. Like I said, I'm sure that it is only from my perspective, but even today I sense that I'm not as outgoing or as friendly as I once was. Many times, I try to ease out of any crowd, including church, without facing too many people.

My church has always had my back, as the saying is today. They have been very supportive, never openly judgmental, and I say that cautiously because I know several people in 1992 when I went nuts were thinking judgmental thoughts for sure. I know I would have been.

I think any Christian needs a family based church to receive weekly strength from, just being among fellow Christians. I have witnessed to people in the past that proclaim that they don't need to go to church. They say they can be just as religious out in the woods or wherever. To me, that is not true. They can't draw strength from their friends that are concerned, or hurting themselves. They can't hear those outstanding testimonies that someone has come through the fire and hear people tell how God saw them through the tough times.

I've heard people use the excuse that they weren't going over there at that church because of the hypocrites in the church. When I was younger, I have even heard my daddy make statements like that, but we had a pastor of our church once make a statement that I will never forget. I probably disliked him as a pastor more than any we've had, but his comment was this:

> "If a hypocrite is standing between you and God and preventing you from worshiping God, then that hypocrite is standing closer to God than you are."

It's ironic that I didn't like the preacher very well, but his statement has meant more to me than some others throughout the years. When you really think about it, his statement is very true.

Over my lifetime I have always been pretty faithful to attend church, but I am living proof that even if you're sitting on a church pew every Sunday, doesn't mean that your living like God wants you to. I've felt just about as low and as corrupt sitting in church, than someone that was hung over from a night out. Guilt and shame attack us all if you have a conscience, and if you're a Christian God will convict you of your shortcomings.

God says there is no sin bigger, or worse than another, so that means that if I have a jealous thought, a selfish thought, or a lustful thought, that is a sin. No better nor worse than someone that committed adultery, or murdered someone. We are all sinners, some have just been saved by God's grace.

I have enjoyed attending my Sunday school class for the past several years. I haven't always appreciated attending at certain times throughout my life. Some points in my life I went just because I felt obligated.

We now have a man in our Sunday school class that is a true blessing to me. He was raised here just like me, a little older than me. His mother was a member of our church all my life, but he got off on the wrong track several years ago. He got on drugs for several years, then God showed him the way out of that kind of life. He has been attending our church for several years now, and been drug free for several years. He is kinda shy like me, and hates to talk in front of people. I've encouraged him for the past few years to give his testimony in front of our church. He's always told me he doesn't think he can do that, but a few weeks ago he told his testimony to our Sunday school class. I really was blessed. I still love to hear profound testimonies of how God has saved people from terrible circumstances. He has a nephew that has a similar track record and he has been clean for twenty five plus years as a recovering substance abuse addict that also attends our Sunday school class. I'm proud of men like those that find their way back out of such a sinful grip.

As you go along life's way, everyone has struggles as they go. I believe that your church family is where you need to go to draw strength. My church family has been a huge support group and that means a lot to me. I am ashamed to tell this, but after 1992 I haven't been very active to serve on committees or such in our church, but the past year I have begun driving one of our church vans picking up little kids. It has been a blessing to me to see those little ones come running up to the van anxious to get on the bus. They seem to be excited about going to church.

I have talked about my friends somewhat, but as far as lifelong close friends, I've had only a few really close friends. Most of my childhood friends that I was really close to when I was in school grew up and we went separate ways. I still have a couple of close friends that goes back to school days, but most of my lifelong friends were established as a young adult. Most of my childhood friends, as well as my really close friends have now passed away. I am very thankful for my close friends for helping my wife, as well as myself, as we went through that period of time in 1992. Close friends are very important I believe, and along with my family members, my friends have helped me throughout my life in different ways.

In this book I have deliberately tried to avoid personal names except for my immediate family, but one friend that I will mention was a special friend. The one person that I spent the most time with over my life's span. He was seven years older than me. He was raised locally and loved to hunt and fish. We started fishing and hunting together in the early 1970s. There was something about our characters that just fit each other. We hauled a fourteen foot flat bottom boat all over the country fishing stock ponds. We hunted deer, turkeys, squirrels, or whatever season was open. We spent hours noodling for catfish along the Washita River and the creeks that fed into the river. We've spent hours fishing for Crappie. We've hunted skunks and hogs at night many times. Anything sporting, he was "all in."

Anything we did, he would make it a challenge. Who caught the biggest fish, or the most. Who killed the biggest deer and such. He would get the biggest kick out of beating me, but he wasn't the best loser. He would pout a little if I beat him, but he would get over it soon. I will admit that it wasn't very often that I beat him either.

Whatever I was doing, he seemed to want to be involved. I've used the remark before that, "I bet we've traveled, in a truck or boat, a million miles together in our lifetime." That is an exaggeration, but we've traveled several thousand for sure. After he retired from his occupation, he would help me build fence, work on my hay baler, or whatever I needed help with. He never would accept any pay, but I always tried to make it right by taking him and his wife out for supper, or I would buy him something to try to equal it out in some other way.

You know you have a true friend when they're willing to work hard just to help you and not expect any pay. We stayed close friends until his death in 2017. What was strange, was the people that didn't know us very well would have thought we almost hated each other. The other church members would look at us so strange when they would hear us going at each other. We would call each other names and talk smack to each other like the other was a sorry dog and such. It sounded terrible to the onlookers, but we were just giving each other a hard time. We both knew what we were doing. That was just our way. Any one that I truly care about, I have to aggravate them and talk trash to them. Ronnie was the same way.

Life has many unexpected turns as you go along. My friend's name was Ronnie, and even though he was seven years older than me he was very healthy, didn't have many aches and pains, and he hadn't had many health issues throughout his life. As for me, I have had nine different surgeries, including both knees replaced. I've had an ablation performed inside my heart for treatment of Atrial Flutter. I've suffered from arthritis since I was thirty years old, so I get around like an old cripple. He could outwork me when we were building fence and such, even at seventy years old. He just had better health than myself, so I always felt like he would out live me.

Over the past few years, he would always make comments something like, "Well if the Lord allows me to live until next February I'll be so old," and give me the number of whatever birthday he had coming up. As he would make comments like that, I would tell him, "yeah you'll live to be ninety since you are so healthy." Then, the unexpected happened. He developed cancer, and within the same year elected to have surgery to better his chances of surviving longer. He didn't overcome the surgery, so his life was cut short. He passed away at the age of seventy two.

You never know what your next stepping stone is in life. For Ronnie, his was his final destination. He stepped into heaven. He went home to be with his Heavenly Father. Ronnie and I drank coffee almost every day for the last six months of his life after he had been diagnosed with cancer, and we had many different conversations about eternal life. The most comforting thing for me, was that Ronnie knew his Savior Jesus Christ personally, and he was prepared to meet him. He made the comment several times in his later days, that whatever God had in store for him was alright with him. He was ready to meet his Lord. He said, "I'm a winner either way." I know he meant every word.

Ronnie had tried his best to keep the holes repaired on our local bridge called "The Greasy Bend Bridge," for the last three years of his life. It was getting old and holes would develop in the floor. The county wasn't too energetic to repair them because they had planned to build a new bridge before long, so Ronnie took it on himself to be the caretaker of that old bridge, so I would go help him patch holes and such at times.

That old bridge had a special meaning to Ronnie. His father had helped build it many years before, and he crossed that old bridge almost every day of his life. He was raised across it from our local town, and after living a few other places in his younger married life, Ronnie and his wife had built a home on his parents old home place, so again he had crossed it almost every day for the past forty years of his life. A few years ago, Ronnie wrote a poem about that old bridge, about it being built by just common working men, which included his father. The bridge had a special place in Ronnie's heart.

This picture was taken standing on the new bridge.
It's a picture of both the old Greasy Bend bridge,
the one that Ronnie was so fond of, and the new one.
They built the new bridge beside the old bridge. Ronnie
didn't live long enough to get to cross the new one.

They started construction on the new bridge just as Ronnie began treatments on his cancer. Ronnie passed away before the construction was completed, so he never got the privilege to cross the new bridge. Some of us local people solicited the county commissioner to name the new bridge as a memorial bridge for him. He agreed, and when the construction was completed we had a dedication ceremony for dedicating the bridge as his memorial, and they put signs at both ends. It was named, "Ronnie Colbert Memorial Bridge."

That made several people in the community happy, including Ronnie's wife. We all felt like it was very deserving of him.

Like me, Ronnie cared about the simple things of life and was willing to spend lots of hard work, sweat, and his own expenses to keep that old bridge in good condition.

Ronnie was our song leader at the Mannsville Baptist Church for well over thirty years. He loved the Lord and loved serving his church. He had a compassionate heart and I will always be grateful for having had the privilege of spending so much time and joy with him.

My oldest brother Carl and I, as I have mentioned before, have always liked to travel to other states, to hunt or just take trips together. Both of us have traveled to several states on our own, and some together. In 2013, Carl's son-in-law had built a tool trailer and sold it to an oil company. He hired Carl to deliver it to North Dakota, so Carl called me and ask if I wanted to ride along. We decided at that time that we would make an agreement to try to visit all of the lower forty eight states before we got too old. This was trip number one. We left Oklahoma and went north, across Kansas, Nebraska, South Dakota and on to North Dakota, delivered the trailer, then went on west into Montana, Wyoming, Utah, and several other states before we came back home.

In 2014, I had a trailer built in Georgia, so we decided to go on our second trip to include several more states as we traveled to go retrieve that trailer, instead of having it delivered here. We left home and went east through Arkansas, Tennessee, then Kentucky before turning south into Georgia. We picked up the trailer, came back along the southern coast line and traveled through more states coming back home.

In 2015, we booked a guided bear hunt in Montana in the month of May, so we left here a week before our bear hunt was scheduled, in order to travel to the west coast and cover more states. We traveled straight west across New Mexico, Arizona, and then went through California, stopping to see the Redwood and Sequoya trees. We then continued north into Oregon and Washington, then across Idaho, ending up in Montana just in time for our bear hunt.

During this trip we had gotten to Spokane, Washington late one night, needing a place to stay for the night. I started calling motels. All the motels were full because of a huge college graduation in that town. Being that I am a southern farm boy, I have a distinct southern draw about my voice. I've had people comment on how much of a country hick I sound like, even in my home town. Nevertheless, after calling several motels without finding any vacancies, I called the Holiday Inn at the airport. The lady on the other end of the phone was very friendly. She told me they didn't have any rooms available, nor did any other hotel have any rooms available and told me the reason, so I begin to question her, asking if she had a cot we could sleep on, or anything. I told her we were desperate and needed a place just to lay down a while, that we'd been driving for fifteen hours. She began laughing and ask if we would be willing to sleep in a conference room on cots. I told her, absolutely. When we got to the registration desk I ask her why she was so accommodating? Her reply, as she was laughing, was, "I'm a sucker for a Hillbilly." She had her maids fix us up in a conference room and set up cots, and we stayed there that night. We didn't sleep much because it was very uncomfortable, but at least we got out of the truck for the night. The next day, we traveled through Idaho and on to Montana, spent a week hunting bear, then started home. We came back through the other states that we hadn't visited before to complete all of the states from home to the west coast.

When I left home, something unusual would almost always happen at home. On this trip we were gone almost two weeks. When we left home it started raining and we ended up having one of the worst floods in my home town of all times. The rain washed out gullies from underneath my fences. Trees fell down across some of my fences, so I want to thank my two sons for keeping a watch out, as well as repairing things during that time. They both had to rebuild fences and build barriers on gaps under fences, and multiple things to prevent my cows from getting out. It seems like it would never fail, when I left home things like that would start to happen. On another one of my hunting trips, before leaving home I had ask a good friend to watch after my cattle. The friend that had been my partner in the hog business. After I left, my young calves started getting sick. It took my friend, my youngest son, my middle brother Lyndal, and his son to keep those calves doctored until I got back home. I'm very thankful for all those men for helping me in times of need. It is good to have friends and kinfolks living around you to help out at times. I appreciate them more than they know.

In 2017, my brother and I only lacked the northeastern portion of the United States to complete all forty-eight states, so we headed straight east into North Carolina, then turned north, covered all the states on the east coast, went through New York City then onto

Maine, and finally turned back southwesterly. We spent one night at Niagara Falls. If you haven't been there, I would encourage you to go, but the most impressive part was the very tall tower across the Canadian border. It has a revolving restaurant in the top of it. As you ate your meal, the floor you were seated on was turning very slowly. We made a complete revolution during our meal. It's something to see if you ever go into that area. We left there, dropped southwesterly across more states and into Ohio, then turned straight north to go up into the upper peninsula, between two of the Great Lakes, then back west. We came back through the remaining states that we hadn't visited before, to complete our mission we started five years earlier.

We have driven through all forty eight states, but when I say that, let me paint you a picture. We leave home with limited amount of days to be gone. We drive like maniacs into, and through all these places. We cover an average of seven hundred miles a day, so to say we have visited all forty eight states is deceiving. Most of the time we were just catching glimpses of things as they go by. Those forty eight states have just become a blur in my memory except for a few particular places, but we accomplished our task. We have been in all forty eight states.

On our Montana bear hunt in 2015, we didn't harvest a bear, actually didn't even see a bear except when we came back through Yellowstone National Park where we saw a grizzly. Carl still wanted to kill a black bear, so in the fall of 2018 he and I booked a bear hunt in Ontario, Canada. We left Oklahoma a couple days early so we could travel north up into Canada a ways and across Canada for a few hundred miles before reaching our bear camp. We were successful in both of us harvesting a black bear, then true to our track record we came home in record time as hard as we could go. It's a wonder they didn't throw us under the jail, because we didn't drive the speed limit much of the time. We left the bear camp about lunch and I told the other bear hunters that we'd be home by midnight the following night. We spent the night in Minnesota within a few miles of the Canadian line. We left there the following morning at 7:30 a.m., and I think it was 1:30 a.m. when we actually got home. We had traveled

930 miles that last day. It was a long, long day, but we were only one and a half hours later than I had predicted the day before.

There is an inside joke I need to insert here. My brother Carl is a unique person. As long as you're going away from home and making your trip, he's fine, calm and casual, but he's like an old barn sour horse when you start heading back home. He can't wait to get home and he'll drive all night to get there when it's time to go home.

Back to my life's journey, by 2014 or so things begin to become more constant or consistent in my life. I truly felt relief that our retirement wouldn't be as gloomy as it once would have been. I felt like a man that had been brought through the fire and even though I had scars on me, God had seen me through to a better place. The feeling of accomplishment, if you will. We were heading toward retirement with the vehicles in place, and with God's blessings they could grow with us as time went along.

By vehicles, I mean we had done our due diligence to get the minerals bought, and the oil companies were still continuing to drill more wells. The minerals that we had bought, as well as the ones we already owned, were coming into productions. I began to look behind me again at this stage of my life and actually marveled at the things that had happened only in the past ten years of my life. Things that I couldn't have even imagined ten years earlier. God was showing me his power in a miraculous way. Most of the local people, including me, had no clue that oil and gas even existed in our area.

I will say at this point, that my wife and I will never be wealthy because of the mineral interest we own. We don't own much, but the revenue that we will receive from that will certainly help extend our Social Security checks. They are a true blessing from God, that we wouldn't have received any other way. I haven't told about the minerals in a boastful manner at all. I wanted to tell my story how God used those minerals to help my wife and I to sustain a reasonable income throughout our retirement.

God will find a way to provide for his children if you'll seek his leadership. I was worrying myself sick only ten years earlier, about how we would sustain a certain standard of living after we retired. God bringing forth the mineral production in our area was not just out of luck. He planned it that way. It has helped my siblings, my friends and neighbors. Most of those people are good hard working people. God blessed us all.

Rylee with one of her deer. She has killed several deer up to date.

The grandkids liked to hunt, so between me and their dad one of us would take them deer hunting each year. Naturally, Rylee started a few years ahead of Dillard. They each started when they were probably ten or eleven years old. They have both killed several deer each, now. Of course I tell them it's because they had good guides with their dad and I.

Dillard with one of his many deer. He's killed more deer before he was 16 than I had at 25 years old.

Rylee was about to start high school, with Dillard three years behind her. Rylee was playing every kind of sports she could, and by then Dillard was playing basketball, track, and a little football.

The way the schools do now, is if their school was playing another school, the boys would play in one of their locations, while the girls would play in the opposite. So for the next few years, many times I would go watch Dillard, while Debbie would go watch Rylee. The next game, we would switch things around and I would go watch Rylee while Debbie would watch Dillard. We felt like it was necessary to keep it somewhat even between them. The grandkids call Debbie "Ma." It made it tough for me and Ma. We would have both liked to have watched both of their games, but that wasn't possible.

During Rylee's freshman year of high school, her mother found a national data website that you could pay to enter a young athlete into. That website would allow college coaches to be able to go onto that site and watch any kid on it throughout their high school playing activities to see how they might develop, so we paid to get Rylee entered into that database. Rylee and her mom would have to send in clips from some of her games periodically for the college coaches to view.

I was still selling real estate, cutting and baling my hay, and raising cattle while Debbie was still working at her job. Things were finally running pretty smoothly. During this period, for the first time in my life I was pretty stress free. Of course there are always things in our personal life pertaining to our family that would cause stress, but as far as my livelihood, I didn't stay awake at night trying to figure out how to make things work. It was pretty peaceful.

Rylee ran a lot of different events in her track and field career, but in her junior year of school she began jumping the long jump during the track meets for the first time. She wound up qualifying for the state meet. She ended the season standing fifth in the state in her division, which was gratifying for her since she hadn't even tried jumping until three months earlier.

Dillard also ran track, but Dillard wasn't interested in beating anyone. I watched him run races where he would be ahead of another kid, and he was so soft hearted that it appeared to me that Dillard would slow down to allow the other kid to get ahead of him. Now I'm not talking about for the win, but just back in the line. He didn't want to hurt anyone's feelings. Not just because Dillard is my grandson, but he is the meekest, most mild mannered, soft hearted, and most compassionate boy I've ever been around. He is the sweetest kid I could ask for, in a grandson. Dillard didn't have the drive to be number one, or want to be better than someone else. He seemed to be content just being a participant. He wanted to be part of the team, I think mainly because all his best friends were playing sports.

He would amuse me sometimes to watch him. He played football one season, I think his eighth grade year. He didn't play much, but when he did play he would play as a wide receiver, I think. Keep in mind, I don't know much about football. We didn't have football offered at my school when I was in school but nevertheless, Dillard would line up against another kid on the opposing side, and when the snap happened they would do a little tug of war between the two of them. If the other kid hit the ground, Dillard would always offer him a hand to get him up. Me and Ma thought that was really sweet. Not typical of a rough and tough football player, but that was our Dillard. He was always considerate of others.

By his sophomore grade in school, which is the time frame that I'm writing this book, he has quit all sports and is just concentrating on his school work. He is very smart on computers and video games. I'm thinking that he might possibly make his living in that vocation in some way. I have a strong feeling that God has something special in mind for Dillard. He has such a warm compassionate heart and seems to care about everyone around him. The future is still ahead of him, but if he will keep his nose clean and seek God's leadership, God will bless him.

Rylee continued to play softball, run track, jump long jump, and play basketball throughout her high school days. She was honored in her senior year along with other awards, with the MVP award of her basketball team, and I think that award is one of her most cherished accomplishments up to date.

Rylee graduated from high school this past summer and I wrote her a letter about life. That's the way that I communicate with the people I love, so it will be something they can keep, as well me being able to review it myself and make corrections before I present it to them. Anyway, in her letter I tried to introduce her to the real world and have her look at life like a journey. Life has many happy experiences, lots of love if you're raised in the right family, but it also has many valleys, sad times, depressed times, and hills and curves. It will take you to places where you don't ever know what to expect around the next bend and that is how I relate my life to look like back through time. A journey that has lead me into new horizons and different directions over the years, to end up at the present time of writing this book. Even today, I'm sixty six years old and I've seen lots of different things and changes in my life, and if God is willing to leave me here several more years I will see many more, I'm sure.

Rylee's childhood dream was about to come true. She had worked very hard in order to become a good basketball player, so now she was about to reap the reward for all that hard work. The data website that we paid to have her entered into in her freshman year paid off. In her senior year, she had multiple college representatives contact her to come visit their campus. One that she visited impressed her as a good fit. She visited Southwestern College in Winfield, Kansas. She liked the campus and the coaches, so she committed to play basketball for them. She received a scholarship and started going to school there the fall after graduating high school.

My wife, Debbie, got to retire this past summer, just in time to travel some, and just before Rylee graduated high school, and I have taken a break from selling real estate myself. Our intentions are to travel to watch Rylee play college basketball as often as we can, as well as spend as much time as possible with Dillard.

The fall of 2018, Rylee began her college career. She started playing ball pretty soon and true to my oath when she was born, me and my wife have been to several of her games. It is a four hour drive from our home to her school, and with me still feeding cattle and taking care of my farm, it's not practical to make them all, but we have driven that four hour trip as many as three times in one week, a couple different weeks this past winter. We travel that trip at least once every week to watch her play ball.

She has just played her last game of her first season as a Lady Mound Builder. She plans to stay in that school, play basketball, and receive a degree. This is her first year of college, but like her brother, she is a sweetheart. She has a very compassionate heart. She has a lot of drive and determination to achieve things. She wants to be the best she can be in whatever she attempts. I know God has a great future planned for Rylee as well, if she will seek his leadership.

My son and daughter-in-law divorced when Rylee was five years old, so my grandkids were raised, for the most part, about fifteen miles from our house. I want to give a very sincere thank you to my ex-daughter-in-law and tell her how much I appreciate her. She has never tried to keep us from seeing the kids, she has invited us to their birthday parties, and encouraged us to participate in everything they had going on throughout the years. She has been extremely generous in that way. We have had a very good relationship with her. I want to thank you, Jennifer.

I can honestly say, that I believe that both the grandkids have wanted us around, and enjoyed us being there through it all. Even with Rylee being four hours away, she still texts or calls and asks if we're coming to her next game. I think it has meant a lot to them, as well for Ma and Papaw to be available and wanting to share in their lives.

If I pass away tomorrow, I can truly say that God has blessed me with two of the most precious grandkids in the world.

I want them both to know that they have meant the world to me, to get to share in their lives. They gave me a newness of life when they were born, a reason and a real joy to go through life from that point on.

I hope to see many more birthdays and events with them, but only God holds that knowledge. It has been a blessing to share everything with them up to this point.

I feel like I've had a hard life in some ways. Many times throughout my life I have faced many adversaries, hard times, and times when things looked very bleak, but the feeling of joy, peace and contentment that I have in my heart today has made it all worthwhile. God has brought me to a peaceful spot in my life.

People have asked me the question in times past, "what would I have done differently if I could go back in time and do it all over again."

I know that I could have, and should have made different decisions at times throughout my life, because hindsight is a perfect vision. I wished I would have been smart enough to treat my wife and kids different. I could write another book on mistakes I made in those areas, but on the other decisions I've made, I truly believe if I had done things differently, I couldn't have experienced some of the blessings that God has shown me, so I always tell people that ask that question, on areas other than my family, I don't believe I would have changed a thing.

It's been difficult, heartbreaking, and emotionally draining at times, but now looking back, most of those periods of my life was lessons that I needed to be taught.

I truly feel that I had to live my kind of life in order to see the miracles of God throughout my years of travel. It has been a real journey, and I feel very blessed to have been a part of it all.

I prayed over my computer before I ever wrote the first word of this book, and asked God to anoint this book with his blessings so it could be used to glorify him as a finished book, and because of the effects and emotions I've experienced by writing this book and feeling the Holy Spirit as I've worked on it, I have rededicated my life to my Lord and Savior Jesus Christ for his service in whatever capacity he holds for me, as well as a new dedication to my beautiful wife, whom I have not always treated with as much respect as I should have.

I had made a statement earlier in this book, that I didn't really feel like the episode that I had in 1992 was really for my benefit. As I have written this book and took my memories back in time throughout my life, it has made me realize many mistakes I've made, and many misunderstandings I've had with loved ones. The experience of writing this book has been a healing process within itself for me. I know now, that was part of God's plan all along. I can honestly say that the episode in 1992 was to a huge extent for my benefit, as I look back on it now.

I grew a facial beard last fall. I told my wife several months earlier, that if God allowed me to live to be sixty six years old, I was going to quit shaving. My beard is about six months old now.

Some people think that I have just became too lazy to shave. I have never told anyone the real reason I've grown it before now, not even my wife.

When I look at this gray beard, it is a symbol. A sign of accomplishment, if you will. It tells me that I have made it to retirement, which means God has seen me through all the different twist and curves of my life, the hardships and trauma, and I have arrived in a much more peaceful place.

God is so good. I hope the readers of this book can realize what God is doing in your life. I would encourage you to start looking behind you at the things that "just seemed to work out." That wasn't just luck, God has been clearing your path as well.

The previous paragraph was the end of my book, but true to the essence of this book, God is always delivering a new era of life.

This book contains many different phases of my life and many changes that have come about throughout my journey. God is still at work.

I had completed my book about February 18, 2019. My wife and I had just been looking it over and making corrections, when on February 21, three days later, my youngest son, Nathan, came walking up on our porch with an eleven month old baby boy in his arms.

He introduced this baby as our newest grandchild. He had just recently found out that he was the father of this baby.

What was ironic, was that my wife had been hanging pictures of the family on our walls within the two weeks prior to this time. While doing this, as she was coming through the living room one day, she made a statement to me. "I sure do miss having little babies crawling in my floor."

This little baby boy is the sweetest natured baby I've been around, seldom cries at all and he is so pleasant to care for. We've had the privilege to keep him a few days so far. We have just began to get acquainted with him, but he is a true blessing from God.

This is Josue, (Sway) we have just met him, and he is another precious gift from God like my other two grandchildren. Ma got her wish because God sent her a baby to care for and play with.

My prayer now is to get the opportunity to help raise him and influence him in a positive way and possibly lead him to know Jesus Christ as his personal savior someday.

The future for our family has a newness of excitement with this new baby in our family. Ma is very excited that God heard her comment and sent her a new baby to care for. Life is full of surprises and changes. This precious new life that God has delivered to us hopefully will bring joy and pleasure to Ma and me for many years to come.

I am hopeful that God will allow me to live for a while and enjoy this new grandson as much as I've had the privilege to enjoy my other two grandchildren.

"The Lord is my light and my salvation—whom shall I fear? The Lord is the stronghold of my life—of whom shall I be afraid?" (PSALM 27:1).

SUMMARY

What I hope I can relay in this book to a big extent is, whatever your life's journey involves, God is there for you riding along all the way if you'll let him into your life. There are so many little things in my life that I would be worried about at the time and struggling how to do something, or what to do next, and it just seemed to work out much smoother than I ever could expect. Some people will never see that part of what God can do for you. He wants to help us with the little everyday things, not just when you have a loved one sick, or you have some kind of catastrophic event in your life. God has brought me so many little blessings every day that I am so thankful for. He's working overtime in each of his children's lives to smooth the path. He places things, events, and people in our lives to help us along the way, and even sometimes changes the direction we are trying to go, because he knows it's not best for us.

Don't misunderstand what I am saying. We are all going to have hardships, God won't make your life without problems, but he will help you along life's journey and help you through those hardships. My belief is that God allows us to experience hardships and trials to test our faith, and at the same time teach us important lessons about things, but after that event is over, I believe that is a stepping stone for growth in faith. We have to have hard times, and experience certain tragedies in order to grow in our Christian walk with God.

Everyone has a journey to follow, and each one is different from the others, but if you will seek God's guidance the path will be much smoother.

Looking back over my life, I realize just how much God did for me without me even knowing it was him at the time. He has provided doors to open for me that was impossible to accomplish myself. Some of them, I still don't know how it could have worked out like it did. God is so good.

I am a simple man. I don't claim to be very knowledgeable about the Bible, and I can certainly testify that I've not lead the best Christian life, but I know God has directed me to go, and do, and gave me inspirations to turn different directions throughout my life. I know God has been a major part of my life and where I am, and what I have become, without a doubt, is directly because of his direction, his inspirations, his impressions, and his Grace throughout my life.

Looking back through my life, it reminds me of taking a journey, going up hills, down hills, around a curve, and making the next turn, never knowing what you're going to find, or have to face with the next step. I have done a lot of different things for a while, but then that avenue would close and God would lead me into the next phase of my life. These transitions or plateaus of my life are what I refer to as stepping stones. He has placed several different stepping stones in my path for me to follow. Many times while I would restrain against him not knowing what was going on at the time, and without being aware that God was trying to turn my direction from where I was wanting to go until sometime later.

A couple of Bible verses I'd like to reflect on tells us that each of us has a designed purpose for our lives.

> "But I have raised you up for this very purpose, that I might show you my power and that my name might be proclaimed in all the earth." (Exodus 9:16)

> "For I know the plans I have for you," declares the Lord, "Plans to prosper you and not to harm you, plans to give you hope and a future." (Jeremiah 29:11)

Everyone has a journey through life, designed for them. What you do with your journey, or if your conscience enough to recognize that it is God trying to help you along your path, is up to you.

This book represents a large portion of my life and the struggles I've faced, and again, I would like to repeat at this time, I feel like a man that has been brought through the fire. God has brought me through many hardships in my life to end up where I am now. I'm in a sweet spot at the present time of my life. I understand that I am coasting toward my end time on this earth, but thanks to God I'm enjoying my journey better now than most any other time of my life. Whatever time I have left, I pray God will let me enjoy my family, and the simple things he has provided for me and my wife, but when this earthly life is over the most rewarding part is knowing the best is yet to come. I know where I'm going when God calls me home. I'm going to be with my Lord and Savior, Jesus Christ to live through eternity.

If you are having struggles and hardships, and if you would like for God to help you, all you have to do is ask for his leadership.

If you have never accepted Christ as your Lord and Savior, now is a good time to make that profession. It is a very simple process, but you have to be very sincere.

All you have to do is pray to God and acknowledge that he is the King of all Kings, that you believe his son Jesus Christ died on the cross for your sins, admit that you're a sinner, and ask him to cleanse you from your sins and become your Savior.

God is wanting to be your friend. Just ask him for guidance.

> For God so loved the world that He gave
> His only begotten Son, that whoever believes in
> Him should not perish but have everlasting life.
> (JOHN 3:16)

> Jesus said unto him. I am the way, the truth,
> and the life. No one comes to the Father except
> through me. (JOHN 14:6)

ABOUT THE AUTHOR

Weldon Keith Barnes is a first-time author. He is a third generation farmer-rancher, still operating portions of the land his father, grandfather, and uncle farmed. He's a husband of forty-seven years, father of two children and three grandchildren whom he loves beyond measure. He is a perfectionist in anything he does. He believes that working hard will always pay off in whatever you do. He has the ability to build tools and modify equipment to serve his purpose in a better way. He is a faithful member to his church. In his spare time he enjoys hunting, fishing, and spending time with his family. He and his wife Debbie reside in Southern Oklahoma on the land that he loves so much.